THE MYTH OF
HIDDEN ECONOMY

THE MYTH OF THE HIDDEN ECONOMY

Towards a New Understanding of Informal Economic Activity

PHILIP HARDING AND
RICHARD JENKINS

OPEN UNIVERSITY PRESS
Milton Keynes · Philadelphia

Open University Press
12 Cofferidge Close
Stony Stratford
Milton Keynes MK11 1BY

and
242 Cherry Street
Philadelphia, PA 19106, USA

First Published 1989

British Library Cataloguing in Publication Data

Harding, Philip
   The myth of the hidden economy: towards a new
   understanding of informal economic activity
   1. Black economy
   I. Title   II. Jenkins, Richard
   339

   ISBN 0-335-09923-8
        0-335-09922-X (paper)

Library of Congress Catalog number available

Typeset by Gilbert Composing Services
Printed in Great Britain by Biddles Limited,
Guildford and Kings Lynn

CONTENTS

ACKNOWLEDGEMENTS

This book derives originally from a literature survey commissioned by the Policy Planning Research Unit of the Department of Finance and Personnel, Northern Ireland. Their financial support made possible Phil Harding's appointment as Research Officer for a short period and the preparation of a first draft report which was a distant but definite relative of the present text. The support of Ronnie Hall and Jerry Harbinson of the PPRU was particularly helpful, as were the critical comments of a number of their colleagues within the Northern Ireland Civil Service. A specifically Northern Irish publication, *Informal Economic Activity in Northern Ireland: A Review of the Literature*, is available as PPRU Occasional Paper 15, from the Department of Finance and Personnel, Stormont.

Since then the text has expanded and changed in a number of directions. We are grateful to Bill Williams of the Department of Sociology and Anthropology at Swansea for making further funds available for typing, and to Glenys Bridges, Mary Owens and Glenda Saunders for undertaking it with their customary speed and accuracy. John Skelton has, as usual, been a most supportive publisher (and efficient!) and we owe a particular debt of gratitude to the Open University Press's readers, Richard Brown and Jonathan Gershuny, for the helpful nature and encouraging tone of their comments. Any shortcomings which still afflict the text or obscure the argument are, however, solely ours.

Philip Harding
Richard Jenkins

Chapter 1

INTRODUCTION

The notion that all or most modern economies possess, or are afflicted by, a 'hidden' or 'informal' economy, operating alongside or underneath the visible, formal economy, has held policy-makers and social scientists in its sway for some time. It has, in fact, entered into the careless usage of everyday conversation. The potency of the concept can be illustrated by reference to widely divergent examples. Television drama productions such as *The Beiderbecke Affair* or *The Boys from the Black Stuff*, on the one hand, and statements by public figures such as the ex-Chairman of British Leyland, Sir Michael Edwardes (reported in *The Standard*, 30 October 1985), on the other, all contribute to the currency of the 'myth of the hidden economy'. Academic analyses with titles such as *The Hidden Economy* (Henry, 1978) or *Britain's Shadow Economy* (Smith, 1986) serve only to harden this image of the complexities of economic life in the eyes of social scientists, policy-makers and the lay public alike.

The role of professional social scientists – particularly economists and sociologists – in the social construction of a model of 'the hidden economy', has not, however, simply been that of promoting or elaborating upon an already existing idea. As Dr Roberta Miller, Director of the Social and Economic Science division of the American National Science Foundation, has argued, social science created and defined the concept in the first place (*Times Higher Education Supplement*, 14 November 1986). Our argument in this book is that in having done so, in creating the notion of the 'hidden', 'underground', 'black' or 'informal' economy – call it what you will – social scientists have been, and continue to be, wrong in a number of important respects. What is more, their errors are relatively simple to discover and demonstrate. This is what we set out to do in the chapters which follow.

More specifically, this book has three primary aims. First, we have attempted to provide the interested reader with a guide to a literature which is large, still proliferating, complex and often contradictory. We have not, of course, attempted to achieve anything approaching a truly comprehensive coverage. We have, however, discussed all of the major contributions to the literature along with as much of the rest as seemed appropriate.

Second, we have examined critically the various theoretical approaches to the 'hidden economy' and the methods employed in the attempt to document and quantify its parameters and extent. With respect to the drawing of firm conclusions about this literature, we have been handicapped by a number of factors. Most noticeable in this respect is the fact that research into, and theorization about, informal economic activity is characterized by a considerable amount of dissension. Much of this debate is, what is more, couched at a level of lofty theoretical abstraction which renders its translation into testable, 'real-world'-oriented propositions difficult.

The situation is further exacerbated inasmuch as – and the discussion in Chapters 5 and 6 expands upon this in some detail – methodological rigour is conspicuous by its absence in much of the extant empirical work, particularly at the macro-level. As a consequence of this weakness of method, too much of the literature is characterized by an imprecision which, while it may be academically defensible and, indeed, necessary, renders the task of synthesis problematic. Alternatively, as in the case of the early work of Gershuny and Pahl, one finds sweeping and confident generalizations about the nature of changes in patterns of social and economic activity erected on the flimsiest of empirical foundations. As a result of constraints such as these we have attempted to avoid pressing our argument beyond the limits of cautious interpretation and scholarship. We have opted for an approach which presents conflicting arguments and research findings, together with relevant critical comments of our own, in such a way as to allow the reader to draw his or her own conclusions.

This is not to say, however, that we have shied away from mounting arguments or proposing alternatives. Indeed, the presentation of such arguments and alternatives is our third objective. One consistent theme running through our discussion is the need to take seriously actors' perceptions and accounts of what they themselves are doing. In this sense, we ally ourselves to some extent with the theoretical position associated with substantivist economic anthropology (Sahlins, 1974). Further, while we recognize the utility of a broad distinction between the 'formal' and the 'informal', defined with reference to degree of public, typically state, monitoring and regulation, we reject emphatically the notion that the economy of an industrialized capitalist nation can be divided into discrete 'economies', 'sub-economies' or 'spheres' (of either exchange or production). While we recognize the importance of informal economic activities and regard them as central and integral features of 'developed' capitalist economies, we cannot accept the existence of a separate 'informal' or 'hidden' economic domain, somehow isolated or critically different from the economic mainstream. The arguments relating to this issue are to be found in Chapters 3 and 4.

Returning to the problems of method discussed above, it is our view that many of the shortcomings in this respect which we outline in Chapters 5 and 6 derive ultimately from the inappropriate conceptualization of the situation bound up in the 'separate economies' model. Having once rejected that conceptual model, however, we find ourselves somewhat trapped by the language in which the bulk of the literature is couched. We have, therefore, continued, of necessity, to talk about the 'informal economy', the 'black economy', or whatever. This should be borne in mind when reading the rest of the book.

It is not, of course, sufficent merely to criticize. We have also attempted to offer an alternative framework: more flexible than the 'separate economies' model, less dependent upon *ad hoc* classificatory ingenuity, and more reflective of actors' perceptions of the world (and, hence, less inclined to do violence to research findings by attempting to fit them into pre-existing a priori frameworks). Situated within a theoretical understanding of the relationship between the development of the state and formality, and the distinction between 'work' and 'employment' engendered by capitalism, we offer our model – outlined in Chapter 4 and elaborated in Chapter 7 – as a coherent framework for the comparative analysis of informal economic activity in capitalist societies.

The manner in which we distinguish between the formal and the informal, in particular the central role which we, and indeed many other authors, allocate to state regulation as the major criterion of formality, has consequences for the scope of our discussion. Specifically, it is our view that the differences which exist between the planned economies of state socialism, the bureaucratic liberalism of the social democracies of Western capitalism, and the relatively unregulated economies of the 'underdeveloped' or 'developing' nations are not simply differences of degree with respect to formality and state intervention. They are three distinct approaches to the state's involvement in economic life. As such, they are qualitatively different systems. Adopting a substantivist approach in this respect, we would argue that they require correspondingly different analytical frameworks if we are to understand their workings and the relationship between formality and informality in each context. For this reason, we have chosen to concentrate in this small volume upon the industrialized capitalist economies of the West.

Coming back to our opening remarks, if we are right, and the social science community has not only created the notion of the 'hidden economy' but, in doing so, largely been in error, then it is legitimate to ask why the concept arose, and why it has proved so enduringly popular. To start with, we must, of course, acknowledge that the notion was not simply plucked out of thin air. One can trace unbroken, if sometimes weak, lines of direct descent reaching back to wartime notions of the 'black market' (Smithies, 1984), on the one hand, and popular conceptions about the criminal 'underworld' – dating back much earlier to images of 'the world turned upside down' – on the other. Conspiracy theories about secret societies, of which, perhaps, the most notorious is Freemasonry, may also have contributed something to the overall picture.

Popular understandings of the world such as these did not, however, create the myth of the 'hidden economy', although there is little doubt that they prepared the ground for its development and have been influential in its popularization. In tracing the myth's growth, one can point to a number of factors. Five, in particular, are worthy of brief discussion here.

In the first place, there has been a growing awareness – among academics and policy-makers alike – that the formal national accounting systems which modern states employ to measure and regulate economic activity are inadequate. National balance of payments accounts or estimates of the Gross Domestic or National Product are now widely recognized as underestimates of the actual level of economic activity. There have, therefore, been attempts to measure the size of the economy more adequately and to develop theoretical models which encompass or allow for the missing elements. Hence, the 'hidden' economy.

Second, in the 1960s and early 1970s there were a number of strands of theorization and research in social science which actively promoted or contributed to a general model of the economy as compartmentalized or composed of distinct sectors. Although developed independently of each other, there seems little doubt that they had accumulative and interactive effects in helping to elaborate the myth. One of these was the substantivist critique of formalist economic anthropology, which, in the context of studies of non-Western or 'traditional' societies, introduced the concept of 'spheres' of production and exchange (see the essays in Firth, 1967). Similarly, the notion that Third World cities possessed an important 'informal sector' of casual labour was also influential (Bromley and Gerry, 1979). A casual labour market of a somewhat similar nature has also been identified in eighteenth- and nineteenth-century London (George, 1966; Stedman Jones, 1984). A further influence can also be discerned in the rise of models of the 'dual' or 'segmented' labour market (Doeringer and Piore, 1971; Edwards *et al.*, 1975). Studies of casual work among the urban unemployed, particularly the black urban unemployed, have also contributed to this understanding of the situation, both in the United States (Liebow, 1967) and Britain (Pryce, 1979).

Third, there is also criminology and the sociology of deviance to take into account. In particular, one can point to an increasing awareness of the 'normality' of crime, or, to put it perhaps more accurately, the routine – if often trivial – criminality of much of the 'normal' population. One of the most obvious influences in this respect was Sutherland's work on 'white-collar crime' (1949). Another criminological issue bearing on the same topic was the much-discussed inadequacy of official crime statistics (e.g. Box, 1981:157–207). The overall result of concerns such as these was that sociologists of deviance became interested in a wider range of topics than before: 'hidden' crime or deviance was placed on the agenda.

A similar trend can be traced, fourth, in industrial sociology and the study of bureaucratic organizations. In the 1950s and 1960s, in particular, the informal dimensions of organizational life became increasingly recognized as important and were accepted as a commonplace topic for research (Blau and Scott, 1963; Gouldner, 1954). In addition to examining the niceties of formal bureaucratic structure and rationality, researchers were also attempting to discover 'what's really going on'.

Finally, it would be unwise to underestimate the importance of rising unemployment in the industrialized, capitalist nations of the West, in providing the social context in which the myth of the 'hidden economy' has developed. Moral panics about 'welfare scroungers', the 'working unemployed', continue sporadically to infest the popular press. Government ministers and other politicians publicly question the accuracy of the unemployment figures. Many of the unemployed are, it is argued, not 'really' unemployed. The political mileage to be made out of such arguments should be obvious. Academics have also, albeit perhaps for different reasons, expended a considerable amount of time and effort on such questions. In this respect, many sociologists, for example, were concerned to understand what they saw – and, indeed, still see – as long-term shifts in the nature of society. Notions such as 'post-industrial society', 'the leisure society' or 'the information society' may be highlighted as summarizing something of the flavour of these debates.

None of these five factors was systematically connected in the development and articulation of the myth of the hidden economy. There was no shared programme uniting the multitude of contributors to its creation. There was, however, a homology of theoretical approaches or models, and a common set of concerns. It was out of these that the myth – or more correctly, perhaps, the myths – of the hidden economy grew. It is with those myths that the rest of this book is concerned.

Chapter 2

Work, Employment and Economic Activity

There is in the advanced industrial societies of the West a moral consensus about the positive virtue of employment and a correspondingly negative evaluation of unemployment. Behind this consensus lies a variety of meanings attached to work and employment. We need at this point, therefore, to develop a clear view of what we understand by the terms *work* and *employment* as they are used in this discussion. The literature on the 'informal economy' is fraught with terminological confusion; this is one feature of the debate to which we do not wish to further contribute.

To take a relatively simple example, the difficulties in this respect are nowhere more apparent than in the way in which the size of the civilian labour force is calculated in Great Britain. To maintain consistency in the official labour-force statistics, it is important that all individuals are classified as either 'economically active' or 'economically inactive' (*Employment Gazette*, 1986:21). At either end of the definitional continuum there is no problem. Those people who are in full-time or part-time employment, or who work on their own account, are unequivocally members of the labour force. Similarly, those people who are not in employment, are not seeking employment and say – if asked – that they do not want a job if one were to be available, are just as clearly outside the labour force.

In between there is, however, a degree of confusion. Those individuals who are not in employment, but are actively seeking a job and are available to commence employment, are considered, for statistical purposes, to be an integral part of the labour force, even though they are not actually in employment or working. As members of a statistical category, however, their identity is neither fixed nor 'obvious'; the definitions of 'seeking employment' and 'availability' are matters of some importance here, and not just to social scientists. Considerable publicity has, for example, attached to the numerous changes which the current Conservative government in the United Kingdom has introduced with respect to the criteria for deciding who shall be included within the labour force and who excluded; who shall be definable as 'really' unemployed and who not.

More generally speaking, from the point of view of our discussion, another important consequence of these accounting procedures is that the population of working age is divided into three crude categories: those 'in employment', the 'unemployed' and those who are 'economically inactive'. The relationship of these labels to 'real life' is a moot point. Work becomes, in these terms of reference, largely synonymous with employment, and employment and unemployment, taken together, with membership of the labour force.

Essential to any discussion of informal economic activity, however, is a view of work which extends beyond its simple commonsensical equation with employment. While acknowledging that there is no consensus among sociologists as to what might constitute a precise definition of the term 'work', Richard Brown, writing of contemporary United Kingdom society, attempts to provide an operational definition. He regards work as,

> a very general, all embracing term, used to refer to all those physical and mental activities which are intended to transform natural materials into a more useful form to improve human knowledge and understanding of the world and/or to provide or distribute goods and services to others, in whatever context such activities are carried out.
>
> (Brown, 1978:56)

For Brown all activity, whether mental or physical, which seeks to transform the environment, whether or not it creates a product to be directly consumed by others, can be counted as work.

This is indeed a very broad definition of work. It is moreover one which would embrace within it many activities which might not be regarded as work by those undertaking them. Gardening, for example, is seen by many gardeners as a leisure-time activity pure and simple (Turner *et al.*, 1985:478). Brown qualifies this view of work, however, by making a distinction between 'work' and 'occupation'. He describes an occupation as,

a socially structured and socially recognised set of work activities, the carrying out of which produces goods and/or services for which others would be willing to pay.

(Brown, 1978:56)

An occupation both locates a person in the socially ordered division of labour and provides him or her with a potential or actual place in the market for goods and services. Brown further distinguishes between occupations which involve the individual in a continuous relationship with an employer who directs and controls activity and for which they receive a wage or a salary, and occupations lacking the employment relationship, as in the case of the self-employed professional or the independent artisan. This latter category is in the minority. An occupation most often involves the employment relationship in contemporary industrial capitalist society.

Brown's definition of an occupation appears to correspond closely to what Turner *et al.*'s informants describe as 'real' work (1985:478). It is paid work, the job. In this context, Brown points out that occupations have been of interest to sociologists not only in terms of their objective characteristics, such as pay and hours of work, but also with respect to people's perceptions of these characteristics. The sociological study of the meanings attached to work has long been dominated by inquiry into occupational identity (Brown, 1985:463). This reflects the structuration of status and identity in the United Kingdom and other industrial capitalist societies in terms of occupation. A job is more than what a person 'does'; in many respects it is also what a person 'is'.

This is not, of course, something which is unique to industrial capitalist society. It has probably been a feature of human society for as long as there has been a significant division of labour (Berger, 1975:166). This recognition of the identity-creating possibilities of occupations is, however, particularly important for our understanding of contemporary Western societies because it is possible, perhaps uniquely possible, to be without an occupation in capitalist society, that is, to be unemployed, which, according to this view, may involve the loss of an important and valued social identity. The concept of occupation should not, therefore, be approached from an economic perspective only. Unemployment involves not only the loss of a source of income but also the loss of a source of identity.

The centrality of the wage-relationship as a defining feature of capitalist society is brought out clearly in the work of Garraty. He points out that the 'truly independent worker' can never be unemployed. Artists and writers may find it impossible to earn a decent living but they are never unable to work at their occupations. Similarly owners of their own businesses such as shopkeepers and farmers cannot be unemployed. He argues that,

> in short, only those who work for wages or a salary, who are at liberty to quit their jobs yet who may also be deprived of them by someone else, can become unemployed.
>
> (Garraty, 1978:5)

Garraty notes further that the term 'unemployment' only came into general usage in the English language in the mid-1890s. Its German counterpart, *Arbeitslösigkeit*, was also rarely used before this time. It is a term distinctively associated with free-enterprise capitalism where employee and employer are not permanently obliged to each other and labour has become increasingly dependent because of the separation of workers from the ownership or control of the means of production. In a capitalist society employment should be understood in terms of the defining relationship between capital and labour, and unemployment seen to be a possibility only for those moving in an economy dominated by the employment relationship. Even public-sector employment, which does not involve the same clear-cut opposition between labour and capital, is defined as a relationship in terms of the axiomatically legitimated dependency and insecurity of 'free' labour in the capitalist labour market.

To return to the definition offered by Brown, quoted above, how useful is such a conceptualization of the relationship between work and employment? Clearly we have here a definition of work which extends some way beyond occupation and employment. Pahl would, however, be of the opinion that our definition stretches too far, pointing out (1984:126–8) that such a broad definition of the term work allows for no differentiation between work and other social practices. Every kind of task or activity could be said to contribute to the production or reproduction of the social environment within which it takes place. Even various forms of recreational activity might be described as work since they can be interpreted as reproducing the employee's productive capacity.

Pahl argues that we ignore the indigenous or 'folk' perceptions of work at our peril. In our view, he is clearly correct. The 'real' work mentioned by Turner *et al.*, (1985) is one kind of work, what Handy (1984:52) describes as 'job work'. But its very description as 'real' suggests that there are in fact other kinds of work envisaged by the actors concerned and capable of adequate description by their day-to-day vocabulary. While Pahl, very sensibly, urges caution in adopting a simple dichotomous typology of work, e.g. whether an activity generates money or not, he also warns against the adoption of an all-embracing definition such as that proposed by Brown, which tends to foster a kind of 'radical functionalism'.

For some commentators, therefore, not all social activity is work. What is or what is not work can only be established by looking at the specific social relations within which an activity is embedded. Work is such a basic concept, in both the vocabulary of social actors and of sociologists, that to define it too precisely, at the expense perhaps of leaving the term with only limited analytic value, is misguided. The notion of an 'occupation' does not, however, adequately fill the gap left by its imprecision. We require some operational criteria with which to distinguish work from non-work. Foremost among these criteria for Pahl must be actors' own perceptions of what they are doing. While employment is one form of work, perhaps the easiest for the sociologist to understand, any discussion of the 'informal economy' must of necessity involve a consideration of work outside employment. Some distinction between work and non-work, outside of the employment relationship, must also therefore be possible. We shall return to this topic in Chapter 8, in our discussion of the notion of 'leisure'. While employment is, for our purposes, a technical term which refers to a relationship specific to a capitalist economic system, the term work cannot be so precisely defined. It is a term firmly contextualized in the social relations which generate it, relations which are not all unique to capitalist society.

At this point it may be worth briefly digressing to make a further point, albeit one which is not of central relevance to our discussion. Having distinguished between work, as a general category of economically-oriented transformative activity, and employment, a specific work relationship associated with capitalism, it is possible also to draw a distinction between 'free' employment and a work relationship which involves working for somebody else in an unfree capacity. Work situations which fall into the latter category include slavery, serfdom, prison labour, indentured servitude, and, certainly until recently in the industrialized societies of the West, female domestic labour. The defining feature here is the legal or customary definition of the relationship which subordinates the worker to the will of a master or mistress. The relationship is qualitatively different from that which exists between employer and employee. Although there is no readily available designation, it seems to us that, bearing in mind the possible confusion arising from the words' more specific usages, this relationship may be described as existing between master or mistress and unfree labourer, in short, as 'bonded labour'.

We thus distinguish between 'work', 'employment' and 'bonded labour'. For the sake of intellectual coherence, and given the constraints of space, we intend to concentrate upon the first two, work and employment. Given the importance of administratively or legally defined relationships and regulation in bestowing either formality or informality upon particular practices, to attempt to do more is beyond the means of this short discussion. As a consequence, however, the scope of the argument is curtailed, in two specific directions. First, this is a further argument for the exclusion of the 'underdeveloped' or 'developing' nations of the Third World *and* the state-socialist countries from our deliberations. While employment, as we define it, is important in both, the significance of various kinds of unfree labour is such as to make it impossible to ignore. Our attention will, therefore, be firmly fixed on the industrialized, capitalist states of the West. Second, within Western industrial capitalism we shall ignore that sector of the workforce which cannot be defined as made up of 'free' employees. This is, in the main part, composed of either illegal immigrants or immigrant workers – such as the 'guest workers' of Europe – employed on tightly restrictive contracts. These, in our view, represent specialized cases, lying largely outside our terms of reference (see Portes and Sassen-Koob, 1987, for further discussion).

Our concentration upon relational, organizational and legal-customary criteria in drawing a working definition between work and employment may seem perverse or less than helpful to some readers. Should not the distinction be between paid work and unpaid work? The former, which embraces employment and self-employment, involves working for an employer or a customer and is fundamentally market-oriented. The latter, unpaid work, encompasses a broad spectrum of activities from domestic labour to voluntary work.

We have adopted our distinction between work and employment, rather than one between paid and unpaid work for a variety of reasons. First, our concern with formality and informality predisposes us to pay attention to the bureaucratic or organizational control and definition of economic activity and economic surplus. Second, we do not believe the distinction between paid and unpaid activities to be either straightforward or self-evident. The use of family labour in small businesses is a good example of this problem, as is the ambiguity of transactions based upon the exchange of goods or services rather than cash. Further support for our argument might also be derived from the domestic labour debate: what is the role of unpaid female domestic labour in determining the wages paid to men in the labour market? Nor, third, are we happy with a clear-cut distinction between those economic activities which are market-oriented and those which are not in terms of remuneration or its absence. It is our experience that the rational calculus of the market – concerned with profit, loss and pricing – is influential in many more transactions than those which are strictly financially oriented. Finally, to reverse the argument, even in those transactions or relationships which are primarily concerned with financial transfers, many other factors (bound up with values, effect or whatever) routinely come into play to influence outcomes. The distinction between the 'economic' and the 'non-economic', while perhaps clear enough in common-sensical terms, should not be taken for granted.

In this chapter, we have attempted to establish that apparently straightforward words such as 'work' or 'employment' must be used with care, and, where possible, precision. Bearing these problems in mind we prefer to use the general expression *economic activity* to cover all the practices and behaviours with which we are concerned in the discussion which follows. It is important to specify the 'economic' dimensions of this activity – defined in the largely commonsensical language of day-to-day life – in order to meet Pahl's criticism that over-general definitions of work as transformative activity go so far beyond the routine, socially shared understandings of the word as to be analytically unhelpful.

Within the context of this broad category of economic activity, and bearing in mind our discussion of the concept of 'bonded labour', we distinguish further between *employment* and *work*, the former being economic activity carried out within a capitalist employment relationship, be it formally or informally organized, the latter – 'bonded labour' apart – being all other forms of economic activity. Around these concepts will turn a major part of the argument in the closing chapters of this discussion. In those closing chapters we shall also return more critically to the distinction between the 'economic' and the 'non-economic'. For the time being, however, we will allow that distinction to stand.

Chapter 3

MODELS OF THE INFORMAL ECONOMY

It may be unnecessary to begin by underlining the obvious point that any discussion of models of the 'informal' economy presupposes the existence of a 'formal' economy to which it relates. It is rather less obvious, however, that an absence of formal regulation is the historical norm. History may be viewed as the progressive encroachment of formality upon widening areas of social life, as a consequence of literacy and the introduction of ever more sophisticated information technology, on the one hand, and the increasing power and bureaucratization of the state, on the other. Each of these historical trends is, of course, dependent on the other. This is a theme to which we will return. Here, however, we intend to concentrate on models of the informal economy which have been generated within a shorter-term perspective.

Given the overall orientation of our discussion, as outlined in Chapter 1, the models considered in this section will generally be those developed with reference to Western industrial capitalist societies. Where the experience of Third World or state-socialist countries is relevant to our discussion, reference may be made to models dealing with these societies. However, no particular effort will be made to present a comprehensive discussion of such models.

The first informal economists

The term 'informal economy' was first developed in a Third

World context (Bryant, 1982). Hart, for example, used it to take account of that sector of the urban economy which did not appear in the national statistics of Third World governments (Hart, 1973). It was thereafter typically used to refer to ways of making a living outside the formal wage economy, either as an alternative to it, or as a means of supplementing income earned within it (Bromley and Gerry, 1979).

It is not surprising, therefore, that the earliest systematic attempt to talk of United Kingdom society in terms of different economies or economic spheres should occur in the work of an anthropologist. Davis (1972) depicts the United Kingdom economy as composed of four distinct spheres, which he refers to as 'sub-economies'. The 'market sub-economy' includes all transactions in services and commodities, and is governed by the laws of commercial trading, employment and labour relations. The 'redistributive sub-economy' is governed by the laws regulating taxation, welfare and public expenditure. The 'domestic sub-economy' is governed by family law in the last instance, although it is more immediately and pragmatically organized by customary norms. The 'gift sub-economy' Davis describes as being regulated by norms of reciprocal obligation. Davis seeks to demonstrate that there are a variety of ways in which individuals can maximize values other than profit – something which anthropologists had long recognized in the non-capitalist world – and that such non-profit relations exist in the developed world also. His work acquired an added significance as the concept of separate economies was adopted more generally in attempts to come to terms with the economic recession and rising unemployment in developed capitalist economies during the late 1970s.

In Chapter 1, we have already briefly discussed the factors which served to generate what we have chosen to call 'the myth of the hidden economy'. Once it had appeared, however, the entry of the concept of the 'informal/hidden economy' into the sociological vocabulary did not establish an entirely novel area of research in the industrial economies of the West. Rather, the notion was adopted to further the conceptualization of processes which were already well documented. Research into the 'informal economy' can, in fact, be related to at least five established areas of academic interest: first, revenue loss as a result of tax evasion; second, the general cost of criminal activity;

third, workplace and occupation-associated crime, particularly 'white-collar crime'; fourth, networks of mutual support among extended kin; and fifth, rising unemployment as a result of the restructuring of capital in Western industrial society. Such areas of research largely predate the academic interest in the future of industrial, capitalist society which became the vogue from the early 1970s onwards.

It is not only academic research interests with which we are here concerned, however. Each of the five areas outlined has its concomitant social or economic policy dimension. The first three may be characterized as primarily concerned with aspects of social control or policing; the other two are more oriented towards issues related to social welfare. The conflict between the assumptions and goals implicit in these two areas of policy can frequently be discerned in the literature.

It was the decline in manufacturing industry in the Western capitalist economies and the accompanying loss of large numbers of jobs which, in the first instance, generated speculation as to the form which capitalist society might take in the future. Bell (1974) predicted the demise of industrial society, characterized by the production of manufactured goods and the employment of the majority of the population in time-consuming, unsatisfying forms of work, and its replacement by a 'post-industrial society' in which the provision of services would be the major labour-intensive economic activity. Bell was basically optimistic about the future for capitalist, post-industrial societies. Information would replace raw muscle-power as the medium of production. Human interaction would increase and the more mundane tasks would be undertaken by machines. Whereas industrial society was defined in terms of a living standard based on the amount of goods possessed, post-industrial society would be defined in terms of the quality of life, measured in terms of access to amenities and services. Tricky questions which were raised by his analysis – such as the basis for the distribution of resources in post-industrial society – were largely left unanswered by Bell.

Much of the optimism about post-industrial society has since been replaced by pessimism, as a consequence of socio-economic developments during the late 1970s and early 1980s. The recession has produced a shift of orientation with respect to issues such as 'the decline of work'. Academic research concerned with the 'informal economy' has uneasily straddled these opposing orientations of optimism and pessimism ever since. Mass unemployment has come to represent a more realistic view of the future for many people than a Utopian post-industrial society.

It is against the background of an existing academic tradition, then, and in the light of conflicting policy concerns and predictions about the future, that research into informal economic activity has proceeded. We shall now examine one of the most influential models of the 'informal economy' to be developed in the United Kingdom context, that of Jonathan Gershuny, tracing its evolution in relation to previous models and describing subsequent models which have been influenced by it, in particular that of Charles Handy. Gershuny's work has been chosen as a stalking horse for the discussion which follows because, the sharpness of our criticisms notwithstanding, it is one of the most sustained, imaginative and rigorous attempts to analyse informal economic activity which we have available.

Gershuny: the elaboration of the model

Gershuny begins with a fairly simple model of the economy, that traditionally used by economists in developed countries. He sees the formal economy as consisting of flows of money and commodities between households and the formal productive system. Households provide labour for the formal production system and, in return, receive money in the form of wages. With this money households buy goods and services from the formal production system. Gershuny decribes these exchanges as 'specific' (1983:33), in that the flow of commodities in one direction is matched by a flow in the opposite direction. The total flow in any one direction can serve as an indicator of the extent of formal economic activity. This is how governments estimate the Gross National Product (GNP).

Gershuny recognizes that there are three types of economic activity which cannot, however, be accounted for by governments in this way. This informal productive activity is of three kinds: the 'household', the 'communal', and the 'underground'. Such economic activities are very different from those taking place in the formal economy. We will discuss each of these three kinds of informal productive activity in turn.

In Gershuny's model, households consume the goods and

services purchased from the formal productive system but they may also use purchased goods as capital with which, in combination with household labour, to produce further goods or services for final consumption. Whereas flows between the household and the formal productive system are specific, inasmuch as they are conditional on the exchange of a commodity for money, flows within households are not based on 'any specific and explicit exchange of definite quantities of commodity' (1983:34). Gershuny suggests that we can distinguish exchanges between households and the formal productive system (which are explicit, quantified and relatively short-term) from exchanges within households (which are implicit, non-quantified and often very long-term or never consummated). It is a distinction between exchanges which are specific and those which are generalized.

The growth in the household economy has been encouraged, Gershuny argues, by the rising cost of purchased services relative to the declining cost of 'domestic capital goods'. He also attributes the growth of the communal sector of the economy to this development. The communal 'sector' or 'productive system' includes a wide variety of activities, from baby-sitting circles to the good works of religious organizations. Money exchange may be associated with certain of these activities but generally 'what distinguishes this category of production is that real money is not used as an indicator of value for value' (1983:35). While certain aspects of the communal productive system have something in common with formal economic activity, as, for example, in those transactions where money is exchanged for services, in many respects communal production has more in common with exchange within the household. This sector is predominantly characterized by generalized exchange.

Gershuny's third category of informal productive activity is the 'underground', 'hidden' or 'black' economy. Like the communal economy, this traverses a continuum between the specific exchange of the formal system and the generalized exchange of the household system, but, unlike the communal economy, it tends to have more in common with the system of formal production: 'In fact it exists in the interstices of the formal economy, consisting largely of economic activities also undertaken in the formal economy often by the same people' (1983:36). It remains separate from the formal economy as a result of the choice of those who participate in it; these activities remain hidden from the state either because they are against the law of the land or in an attempt to avoid taxation or other regulation. While this sector of economic activity has more in common with the formal system, in that exchange is mostly specific and money-based, it has some features in common with the other informal sectors. Gershuny cites the description by Henry and Mars (1978:250) of the generalized nature of certain exchanges in this sphere. Those engaging in the 'hidden economy' often refer to some symbolic and unquantifiable values in explanation or justification of their participation in theft, for example. They might find the activity 'exciting', or are 'just helping a friend'.

For Gershuny, the 'hidden economy' consists of activities which may be classified into three types. 'Type A' activities, such as occupational theft, tax avoidance and taxation evasion, are always associated with formal employment. These activities are differentiated according to the degree of connivance required of the employer. For example, occupational theft is not usually carried out with the knowledge of the employer, while tax evasion more often requires the explicit co-operation of the employer. 'Type B' activities are those which, although part of a formal manufacturing process and, therefore, feeding into the formal productive system, are not themselves a part of that system. Gershuny is thinking here, for example, of the outworker who is employed in the clothing industry and paid low piece rates for work carried out at home. No tax is paid by either employer or employee and the employee is not protected by the various health and safety regulations. 'Type C' activities involve the production of goods and services directly for the consumer, in the form, for example, of house repairs or renovations. Gershuny acknowledges that part of the work done in categories B and C might find its way into the national accounting system as a result of earnings declared in tax returns or spending recorded in household budget surveys.

A view of economic development as a unidirectional process, moving in an evolutionary fashion from reliance on primary production, through manufacturing, to the production of services, that is as a series of major transformations, is rejected by Gershuny in favour of a model which encompasses a variety of smaller transformations between the various economies – the formal economy, the household sector, the communal sector and the underground economy – determined by the particular social and technical conditions extant at any specific time. No one of these various spheres of activity can be understood except in the context of the development of all the others. There is a possible two-way flow between each of the four economies or sectors allowing for a total of twelve potential transformations. Gershuny argues that the household economy has been shrinking throughout the period of industrial capitalism as a result of increased state intervention and the intrusion of the market into its sphere of operation, but that this is not inevitable or historically determined and only took place as a result of specific circumstances. By the same logic it is not inevitable that the amount of economic activity undertaken in the household will continue to decline. In fact, it is Gershuny's thesis that it will increase under present politico-economic conditions.

Gershuny believes that the household and communal sectors have been encouraged in their recent development by the increased cost of obtaining services in the formal sector relative to the reduced cost of purchasing capital domestic goods with which to provide for oneself. There has been a movement of work from the formal economy into the informal economy because it is more economically rational for people to provide services for themselves. It has become more difficult to convince people to obtain private services through the formal system and to pay higher taxes in order to receive more public services. This has meant a loss of jobs, that is 'job work', and increased unemployment.

For Gershuny, the 'hidden economy' consists of activities market' would mean a fall in wage levels as a result of the entry of displaced labour from the manufacturing sector into the labour market, a corresponding fall in the price of services (thus increasing demand in the service sector), and an increase in the labour input per unit of service output because of the lower price of labour relative to capital. However, the United Kingdom labour market does not operate under such conditions. Employment legislation, social security contributions and trade union restrictive practices are all seen as contributing to inflexibility in the formal economy's demand for labour. High effective marginal tax rates, which would result in a correspondingly high rate of loss of social security benefit among low earners, restrict the supply of low-waged unskilled labour. Such imperfections in the operation of the market mean that full employment in the formal economy cannot, under present conditions, be created through reducing wages.

The underground economy is not, however, subject to such exogenous restrictions. The supply of unskilled labour is not uniformly restricted at a time of high unemployment. Where wages are not free to fall in the formal economy, a low-wage informal sector thrives instead. The process is encouraged by the falling cost of certain capital goods which makes it easier for people to own their own tools, making 'own account' working easier and less detectable. The lower costs of working in the informal economy, with its freedom from high marginal rates of taxation and the administrative costs of dealing with the state, may make the transference of part or all of an activity from the formal to the informal sector attractive for some of those working within the formal sector.

This formulation by Gershuny (1983) is the most systematic presentation of the 'separate economies' thesis to date. In the following chapter, we shall consider the wide variety of criticism to which this approach has been subjected. In the remainder of this chapter, however, we shall consider Gershuny's model in the context of those models of the informal economy which preceded it, and the research work which has subsequently been stimulated by it.

Variations on a theme: the proliferation of models

In our introduction to this section we cited Davis's work (1972) as a forerunner of informal economy research proper, and Hart's work (1973) as providing the original central concept for this research. A great deal of research and theorizing was undertaken in the period between the early 1970s and the early 1980s, much of it by Gershuny himself. For a review of this work and, in particular, a classification of the plethora of terms used in the discussion, we are indebted to Stuart Henry (1982). In appraising the relationship between the informal economy and unemployment, Henry develops a typology of 'informal economies' based upon the literature extant at that time.

Henry begins with Ferman and Berndt, who distinguish between the 'irregular economy',

that sector of economic activity that is not registered by the economic measurement techniques of the society but which uses money as a medium of exchange,

and the 'social economy', which is that sector of economic activity,

not registered...and which does not use money as the medium of exchange.

(Ferman and Berndt, 1981:26)

This distinction arose out of a study of households in Detroit. Survey and ethnographic approaches were combined in an attempt to establish the extent to which irregular and social sources were used for obtaining home-related and personal services by households as an alternative to the 'regular economy' (Ferman *et al.*, 1978). They found that 60 per cent of households' services were secured through the social economy as a result of the efforts of friends, relatives and workmates, without any monetary payment. About 25 per cent of all services for which payment was made occurred through the irregular economy. Half the households surveyed had purchased at least one service through the irregular economy; use of the irregular economy did not appear to vary according to income level and participation in the informal economy appeared to be common in all strata of society.

Ferman and Berndt's United States study was carried out at a time when there were increasing attempts to establish the size of the informal economy nationwide. These attempts will be discussed in more detail in subsequent chapters. Henry turns next to the work of Gershuny and Pahl, as they developed Ferman and Berndt's classification. Gershuny (1977, 1978) had, as we have already seen, argued that expenditure on services was decreasing in favour of expenditure on goods. He deduced that people were spending more on manufactured goods so that they could produce services for themselves at home. Burns (1977), on whose work he drew, saw the home as increasingly becoming a unit of production as well as consumption. These ideas were a direct response to Bell (1974) who, as already discussed, predicted that a post-industrial society would see an increase in the provision of services. Gershuny argued that post-industrial society would not be characterized by the increased consumption of services but by increased self-provisioning.

Gershuny and Pahl (1980:7), following Burns (1977), developed Ferman and Berndt's concept of the social economy in distinguishing between a 'household economy',

> production, not for money, by members of a household and predominantly for members of a household, of goods and services for which approximate substitutes might otherwise be purchased for money,

and a 'communal economy',

> production not for money or barter, by an individual or group, of a commodity which might otherwise be purchasable and of which the producers are not principal consumers.

Gershuny and Pahl, this time following Ditton (1977), further introduced the terms 'underground' or 'hidden' to correspond to Ferman and Berndt's irregular economy. We have here the basic tripartite classification of the informal economy used by Gershuny in his most recent model. It was in conjunction with Pahl that he developed the idea of transformation between economies, although at this time he did not emphasize the difference between household and communal economies (compare Gershuny and Pahl, 1979:126, with Gershuny, 1983:38).

Gershuny and Pahl also called for a redefinition of work to take account of activities which were not normally so described. They pointed out that work so redefined did not only occur in the formal economy. Work was undertaken by a variety of categories of people in a variety of different spheres (formal, communal/household, underground) and it should be for research to specify *'which* work in *which* economy for *which* member of the household for *how long'* (Gershuny and Pahl, 1979:134).

Pahl (1980) went on to suggest that an individual's work identity could be maintained when his or her formal employment had ceased if he or she was in possession of certain skills and tools. He suggested that the unemployed were not in such a vulnerable position as they had been in the Great Depression some fifty years earlier. It appeared to be the case that there was a variety of ways of making a living and that participation in the informal economy might prove attractive to those wishing for greater flexibility in the use of their labour and time and searching for greater personal satisfaction in work. Gershuny and Pahl did not, however, go into great detail about the content of their underground or hidden economy. A number of ethnographic studies have been undertaken which specify the processes involved in this type of activity (Ditton, 1977; Henry, 1978; Mars, 1973, 1974; Mars and Nicod, 1984).

Henry (1982) draws attention to the problems involved in using a single term, be it irregular, hidden, underground or whatever, to cover the whole range of activities subsumed under Gershuny and Pahl's definition of,

> production, wholly or partly for money, which should be declared to some official taxation or regulatory authority, but which is wholly or partially concealed (1980:7).

Ditton, for example, argued that the hidden economy, comprising activities such as pilfering, fiddling and trading in stolen goods, was dependent upon some form of formal occupation 'upon which it parasitically feeds' (1977:275). Henry called for a distinction between this kind of activity and 'black' economic activities, such as 'moonlighting' or 'working on the side', which were not dependent upon employment in some formal work situation. His point is that the hidden economy is dependent upon some type of formal employment and should therefore be kept analytically distinct.

Unfortunately, the fourfold classification with which we are left as a result of Henry's review of the literature, i.e. household, communal, black and hidden spheres of informal economic activity, does not correspond to the model which Henry then outlines as a result of this exercise (1982:463). There, he proposes a fourfold classification into 'irregular' (black), 'hidden', 'unofficial' and 'social' (household/communal) economic activity. It is the unofficial economy which is problematic given the previous development of his typology. It is also termed 'informal' by him, a term which he does not discuss in this context, but which he exemplifies, in terms of kind of economic activity, by the 'perk'.

This inconsistency, however, illustrates some of the difficulties inherent in satisfactorily theorizing the relationships between the whole range of activities which are gathered together under the term 'informal economy', a range of activities whose only unifying characteristic appears to be that they do not figure in the accounts of the state. One of the most recent studies to take account explicitly of this aspect of the separate economies model, adopting an approach which takes as its starting point the national accounting problem, is a comparative study of the United Kingdom and West Germany (Smith and Wied-Nebbeling, 1986). The problem of producing anything other than an *ad hoc* model remains clear, however. Such difficulties can be further illustrated if we consider the fashion for dividing the various 'economies' in terms of colour classifications, a fashion that has become increasingly prevalent in recent years. A critical analysis of the logic of the separate economies thesis will be left until the next chapter. Here, we shall move on to look at Handy's model (1984) of the informal economy, which closely resembles that of Gershuny (1983) but which uses a colour-code classification. We must first, however, say a word about the general propensity to colour-classify the various economies.

Further proliferation: the end of the rainbow?

The term 'black economy' has long been in use to describe an area of uncounted economic activity. Its origins as a term are not clear but it is apparently a concept borrowed by social scientists from everyday vernacular usage (an example of which might be the familiar 'black market'). We can only assume that the current trend for conceptualizing various types of economy in terms of colours results from this original labelling. Most recently, Davis (1985:508) has suggested calling all of those economic activities which are recorded in the National Income Blue Books, the 'blue economy', in contrast to the 'black economy' (criminal activities and those activities that would be taxed if disclosed) and the 'informal economy' (all those activities which are neither black nor blue). The practice of colour-coding appears to have reached its zenith (or nadir?) in the work of Katsenelinboigen (1977; quoted by Mattera, 1985:113) who identifies 'red', 'pink', 'white', 'grey', 'brown' and 'black' markets in the Soviet Union. In Handy's work the colour classification is less diverse. He describes United Kingdom society as having 'white', 'black', 'mauve' and 'grey' economies.

Handy is in general agreement with other commentators that 'job work' in contemporary United Kingdom society is changing as a result of factors beyond the individual's control (1984). The world economic recession, technological innovation and rationalization in the business world have changed the employment situation. In keeping with Gershuny and Pahl's earlier observations, Handy recognizes that jobs belong to the formal economy but points out that there is also work in the informal economy. While it is impossible to live completely outside the formal economy it is no longer true that the only world of work which exists is in the formal economy. Handy argues that the informal economy should be seen as a reservoir of labour where 'the unused demand for work ends up' (1984:40).

For Handy, the informal economy has three parts. First, there is the 'black economy', which corresponds to Ferman and Berndt's (1981) irregular, Gershuny and Pahl's (1980) underground or hidden, Henry's (1982) black and hidden, and Gershuny's (1983) underground economies. The 'voluntary economy', a new arrival on the classification scene, is the second component. This refers to all the voluntary work which is undertaken by the population of the United Kingdom. Third, there is the 'household economy', which is equivalent to Ferman and Berndt's (1981) social, Gershuny and Pahl's (1980) household/communal, and Gershuny's (1983) household and communal economies.

Handy sees the 'white economy' (the formal economy made up of the market and state sectors) as operating alongside the black, mauve and grey economies (1984:42). The black economy includes both undisclosed personal services and 'cheating at work'. It is small and illegal. The 'mauve economy' comprises small businesses and personal services operating on the fringes of the formal economy. Such enterprises might develop into a part of the formal economy or may disappear altogether depending upon their degree of success. The 'grey economy' involves domestic activity, which is seen by Handy as the way in which people replace formal economic activity with their own labour, and voluntary work. It is legal and very large. In keeping with the Gershuny (1983) model, Handy argues that the grey economy will grow because of the need to save expenditure by self-provisioning in the home. Handy does not see this growth in national terms only. He anticipates a revolution as a result of which status will be measured in terms of self-sufficiency rather than material consumption. This is an echo of the optimism of Bell's vision of post-industrial society. Perhaps more tellingly, Handy acknowledges that the home will be the only place left in which many people can satisfy their need for work.

The black, mauve and grey economies are, therefore, seen by

Handy as offering opportunities for work outside formal employment. He recommends the adoption of a wider definition of work, taking account of job work (the paid job, including full-time self-employment), marginal work (work done 'on the side', which is sometimes not declared, but should be), and gift work (which includes work done in the grey economy). This particular train of thought can be traced directly back to Gershuny and Pahl (1979).

The problem of consistency in the development of a typology of informal economies, noted earlier with reference to Henry's work, reappears here. There is a lack of correspondence between Handy's three-part informal economy (1984:18–19) and his colour classification of informal economic activities (1984:42). While there is a correspondence between his description of the black economy in both contexts, his earlier voluntary and household economies seem to become subsumed under the term grey economy while the 'burgeoning personal services and home businesses', which we earlier presumed were a part of the black economy, now appear to have a colourful identity of their own, mauveness!

Nor does Handy's colour-code classification correspond readily with any of the typologies developed by the other scholars working in the area. His mauve economy appears to be neither entirely formal or informal. It is a half-way house. Its identification offers the state an opportunity for focussing its attention upon a particularly vulnerable area of economic activity which may move in and out of the formal economy according to financial pressures or bureaucratic and legal regulation, among other factors. By easing the requirements of the state in relation to such economic activities, participation in this sphere may be encouraged and jobs (that is paid work) created.

Handy is, however, clear about one characteristic of his vision of future society. There will be more small businesses, more self-employed, more part-time work, more do-it-yourself and a growth in the black economy. For the individual, longer lives and shorter conventional jobs will mean lower life-time incomes. However, less job hours will mean more discretionary time and the potential for greater personal satisfaction, when measured in non-material terms. The major problem Handy foresees, yet is unable to solve, is the distribution of these goods among the population. Some in society will undoubtedly get richer but the majority will probably be materially poorer. He stresses the need for government action, in both the short- and long-term, to counteract the tendency for polarization among the population.

While there has been a tendency among those propounding the separate economies thesis to offer informal economic activity as an alternative to work in the formal economy, sometimes even as a panacea for unemployment, there has also been a gradual realization that such a view is based on an unwarranted simplification of the situation. As we have noted with respect to Handy's work, there is a recognition that the distribution of economic activity, both formal and informal, is not equal across all sections of the population. While some people may, as Pahl (1980) has suggested, choose particular work styles, the majority of the population are constrained by the socio-economic climate and the availability of opportunities for work. Gershuny (1983) notes that while unemployment may be partially compensated for by 'hidden' economic activity, the informalization of production is unlikely to alleviate it completely. Informal production is an insecure source of livelihood; for most people it is unlikely to be chosen in preference to formal productive activity.

An increasing emphasis upon these kinds of issues has led to criticism of approaches which seek to examine industrial or post-industrial society in terms of the separate economies model. There has been a shift of research attention away from work as an individual activity, undertaken in a variety of contexts, towards the household as the unit of production; a focus upon household work strategies, to use Pahl's (1984) term. This area of research examines critically the relationship between formal and informal economic activity and questions the analytical usefulness of the separate economy model in providing an adequate understanding of the processes of change taking place in contemporary capitalist society. In the next chapter, we shall turn our attention towards the research literature which is concerned with, *inter alia*, the household as an arena of informal economic activity and the substantive and theoretical issues which are raised therein.

Chapter 4

THE FORMAL AND THE INFORMAL

The fourfold classification of economies developed by Gershuny was presented in the previous chapter as one of the most systematic formulations of the informal economies model. We noted that in this model, economic development is conceptualized as a rather less tidy process than is conventional among historians and economists. Economic development, for Gershuny, is the product of social innovation, a series of small-scale transformations of production rather than revolutionary 'great transformations' from epoch to epoch. We shall organize our discussion of the relationship between formal and informal economic activity around a more detailed consideration of his model of these 'little transformations of production' (Gershuny, 1983:38).

Gershuny specifies twelve possible transformations between the different economies. He not only considers the relationship between formal and informal economies but also between informal economies themselves. Here we shall focus on the possible transformations which he outlines between the formal and each of the three informal economies (household, underground and communal). These relationships will be examined in the light of the findings of other studies in order to assess the usefulness of the informal economies model. We shall then discuss a selection of recent work which has been highly critical of the model. Following this, we shall put forward a simple conceptual framework within which, we feel, the relationship between the various forms of economic activity may be better understood and illustrated. To begin, however, we shall discuss Gershuny's view of the relationship between the formal and household economies.

The household in the economic system

Over the last 200 years, there has been a well-documented movement from household/communal production to formal industrial production in the developed countries of the world. This statement is, of course, something of a tautology, inasmuch as it is primarily according to their degree of industrialization that countries are typically described as 'developed' or not. Gershuny argues that the aggregate effect of the many small transformations which have characterized this process of industrialization amounts to the 'great transformation' which figures in the work of many economists, historians and social theorists. As we have noted, however, it is Gershuny's thesis that post-industrial society is characterized by an increasing movement of work from the formal economy back to the household economy.

We said earlier that Gershuny sees the growth in the household economy in recent years as encouraged by the rising cost of services relative to the declining cost of domestic capital goods. He argues that manufactured commodities tend increasingly to be substituted for final services and, consequently, that the share of consumer expenditure devoted to private and marketed services does not rise over time and may actually decline. Driver (1984), using a similar methodology to Gershuny and Miles (1983), an analysis of official agency time-series data, but drawing upon different data sources – United Kingdom input-output data as opposed to European Economic Community data – comes to broadly similar conclusions. Gershuny deals in most detail with the relationship between the formal and household economies, rather than those that exist between the formal and other informal economies, so we will concentrate here on his discussion of factors stimulating movement between these two economies.

Gershuny does not reduce the basis for household choice between formal and informal systems for the final provision of services to their relative price or effectiveness. He recognizes that account must also be taken of the opportunity cost to the household members involved. If a service can be purchased from the formal economy at a price less than it would cost a household to produce it themselves (calculated on the basis of money earnings lost by household members for time spent in informal production, plus the cost of goods and materials used in the informal production) then it is economically rational for the household to purchase that service from the formal economy. Additional hours could be worked in formal economic activity to pay for it. He argues that:

> If the household wage rate is high relative to the cost of services, ... then it will work long hours in paid employment and *buy* services, whereas if its wage level is relatively low it will buy goods and produce its own services (1983:22).

With the decline in cost of consumer goods, and providing relative wage levels remain constant, time spent in informal economic activity becomes more productive, which leads – so his argument goes – to a transfer from formal to household production.

This analysis is, of course, concerned with households rather than individuals. Gershuny argues that it is easier for a household to adjust the total number of hours worked by its members in formal production than it is for an individual. Mixes of full-time and part-time employment are possible among members of a household. Such a view cannot, however, account for the collective behaviour of, on the one hand, households where factors other than economic rationality dictate courses of action, and, on the other, households none of whose members have access to formal economic activity. Consideration must be given to both situations in assessing this aspect of Gershuny's work.

It seems, for example, that Gershuny is too narrowly economistic in his calculation of the relative merits of the differing modes of the final provision of services in either formal or household economies. Factors other than monetary costs should be introduced into the equation, depending on the situation. Pahl (1984:99), writing about the Isle of Sheppey, records that allotment holders not only grew vegetables to supplement their families' budgets, but because of the superior quality of the self-grown product. They also valued the activity as a hobby. It is conceivable, even likely, that self-provisioning of this kind might be continued even if it became economically irrational to do so, because of the benefits to be gained from it in other, non-financial, ways. Cornuel and Duriez, in their study of a French village, note the apparent economic irrationality of certain decisions taken by households in the interest of social cohesion:

> The cost of the network can...extend to a drop in income derived from the formal sector but to counter this there are benefits in the more or less long term. For young householders these are the services which come from the free time which parents have in retirement; for the parents it is the assurance of not being left in isolation. In economic terms, the establishment and evolution of the network can be regarded as an investment which gradually realizes profit.
>
> (Cornuel and Duriez, 1985:173)

This view of economics and 'rationality' is somewhat wider than that implied by Gershuny's understanding of the rationale behind a household's choice of how to obtain final services.

As regards households which have no members in a position to obtain formal employment, and the corresponding redundancy of the notion of opportunity cost as applied to them, the work of Pahl (1984) and Pahl and Wallace (1985) is perhaps most revealing. Pahl identifies a 'process of *polarization* between the busy, highly work-motivated households, generally well off with multiple earners and potential household workers, and others who are at the opposite end of the scale' (1984:218). In many respects, it must be acknowledged that Pahl's Isle of Sheppey findings support Gershuny's general ideas about the current increase in domestic self-provisioning. However, Pahl and Wallace (1985:215) found that employment and self-provisioning went together in Sheppey. The one was emphatically *not* a substitute for the other.

Indeed – and this finding deserves considerable emphasis – Pahl and Wallace found that those without formal employment were actually less likely to engage in informal economic activity of all kinds than those in formal employment. They state that, 'if the sexual division of labour in informal work is taken into account, it is clear...that men who are in employment are more likely to be doing extra work than any other male category and that unemployed men do least' (Pahl and Wallace, 1985:209–10). Similar findings have been reported from the north-east of

England (Morris, 1987:344–5). On the other hand, Gershuny and Miles (1985) report that unemployed men tend to increase their participation in domestic activity following job loss, although they recognize that such participation is the result of necessity rather than choice. Domestic work was no substitute for the satisfaction to be gained from formal economic activity. Increased domestic work reflected the shortages of household equipment and money rather than any renegotiation of the domestic division of labour.

Morris (1985), in a study of redundant workers in South Wales, found that there are powerful social forces which militate against any such renegotiation. She suggests that it is, in fact, dependent upon opportunities for female employment rather than male unemployment. By contrast, Rosemary Kilpatrick and Karen Trew, discussing the lifestyles and day-to-day activities of a sample of unemployed men from Belfast, argue that the amount of work done in the household by unemployed men varies systematically in relation to a number of factors (Kilpatrick and Trew, 1985; Trew and Kilpatrick, 1984). The four lifestyles they distinguish – the 'active', the 'social', the 'domestic' and the 'passive' – each engaged in different amounts of domestic work. This variation appears to be related to attributes such as age and number of children, marital status, occupation and working status of spouse. Findings concerning increased participation in domestic activity due to increased available time, are, therefore, inconclusive. It is possible that regional variations are to be found in addition to variations reflecting other factors.

There are, therefore, obvious problems associated with applying Gershuny's idea about opportunity cost to all households. The usefulness of the opportunity cost hypothesis varies according to a household's position in relation to the formal labour market. Pahl's work suggests that there are an increasing number of households for whom the opportunity cost consideration is inappropriate. The work of Morris and Kilpatrick and Trew in this field introduces a new factor, gender, which is of considerable importance when discussing the opportunity cost of informal economic activity.

Cornuel and Duriez (1985) suggest that women tend to perform more domestic tasks than men because their opportunity cost is lower than men's. The earnings they forgo as a result of productive activity in the household are less than the earnings forgone by men who engage in domestic activity. This is because women are generally paid less than men in the formal economy. Cornuel and Duriez illustrate this point with reference to the fact that the couples in their study who showed most parity in their earnings tended to do similar amounts of domestic work. Morris's findings from Wales, referred to above, would tend to support such an understanding of the situation. Gershuny (1983) is sceptical about such explanations of the household division of labour. He argues that differences between male and female wage rates are more likely to be the consequence of the household division of labour than its cause. Such explanations as that of Cornuel and Duriez he interprets as reversing cause and effect. Whatever the origins of the household division of labour, the differential wage rates of individual members of a household must be taken into consideration when assessing opportunity costs. Differences in wage rates according to age and gender can be expected to affect the structure of particular 'household work strategies' in the light of the relationship between purchase of final services and self-provision outlined by Gershuny and discussed earlier.

Some notion of opportunity cost should, therefore, be taken into account when considering the relationship between formal and household economic activity. It requires considerably more breadth in its operation than is allowed for by Gershuny, however. On the one hand, it is necessary to take account of non-economic, or, more specifically perhaps, non-monetary, factors in determining actors' rationality; on the other, it is necessary to acknowledge the significance of the different positions of households, and of members of households, in relation to the wider social structure, particularly in terms of class, gender, age and access to formal economic activity.

Out of sight if not out of mind: criminal economic activity

We turn now to the relationship between the formal and the underground economies. Gershuny (1983) explains transformations from formal to underground economic activity in terms of a combination of factors. Unemployment, in conjunction with an inflexible formal labour market, the declining real price of capital, the high cost of formal production and the criminalization of particular kinds of formal production, all contribute to the growth of the underground economy. Cornuel and Duriez (1985) outline four basic categories of cost element that promote activities in the informal sector. They are the absence of obligatory deductions from income, such as taxes and social security contributions, the absence of work regulations, the capacity to make quality provision at a price impossible in the formal sector, and the opportunity cost to those participating in it.

The movement of activity from the underground economy to the formal economy is, for Gershuny, the result of full employment, lower tax rates or more effective policing. Cornuel and Duriez also talk of cost elements which are a hindrance or disincentive to informal economy activities. There is the risk, both of personal injury in the absence of safety regulations and insurance, and of the discovery of clandestine activity with the probability of accompanying legal sanctions. There is also the cost of network participation, in that the maintenance of relationships is time-consuming and prevents participation in other activities. There are thus a variety of factors which both promote and discourage participation in the underground economy. Gershuny does not, however, discuss them in as much detail as he does those affecting the household economy. We must look to the work of others for a more detailed account of what is involved.

We have already pointed to Davis's (1972) work as a pioneering development of the idea that the United Kingdom economy is made up of distinct economic spheres (the market, redistributive, domestic and gift sub-economies). Davis sought to establish that the theoretical assumptions of substantivist economics, common in the work of anthropologists studying the 'underdeveloped' world, could provide the basis for an unorthodox analysis of a developed economy. Ditton (1977) and Henry (1978), in particular, took up this anthropological approach in their work on the hidden economy, albeit from differing perspectives in each case.

Ditton accounts for fiddling and other forms of petty theft in the work-place in terms of low wages and work situations where the employee has responsibility for an employer's cash receipts. Particular kinds of industry, for example the service industries, are, therefore, more amenable to hidden economic activity than others. Henry, in contrast, regards such activity as generated by a set of social pay-offs, which are not in themselves economic. The type of industry or job is, therefore, irrelevant for Henry. All employment situations allow potential scope for fiddling. Both writers recognize that there is a complex mixture of economic and non-economic motivations for participation in hidden economic activity. They differ in the relative importance they attach to the subjective explanations provided for their own actions by actors. For Ditton, the economic motive is primary, and non-economic motives are put forward by participants merely to play down the pecuniary advantage to be gained from such activity. Henry, in contrast, treats actors' explanations of their behaviour in terms of economic advantage as erroneous, rationalizations in terms of dominant social mores. He stresses the non-economic dimension of the hidden economy, which he sees as finally determinant. He likens participants' attempts to compete with each other to provide cheap high quality goods from clandestine sources to the *potlatch* ceremony observed by anthropologists among North American Indians towards the end of the last century. The degree to which non-economic or social factors impinge upon economic rationality is the central issue here, as it was previously with regard to the household economy.

One of the present authors has elsewhere criticized Henry's model as particularly inconsistent in this respect. On the one hand, Henry isolates 'discrete spheres of exchange characterised by corresponding domains of discourse' (Jenkins, 1982:5), while on the other, he claims that the cultural pre-eminence of the dominant semantic domain of economic rationality leads actors to misrecognize the 'real' nature of the hidden economy. As a result, they describe its essentially non-economic social relations in the language of the market place. This inconsistency in Henry's work derives from an attempt to fit his data into an anthropological model of economic activity – spheres of exchange – to which it is not suited. As a result of this clumsy anthropologizing, Henry is forced to treat his informants' protestations that they are *really* engaged in economic transactions as 'false knowledge', on the basis of which they attempt to justify their economic 'irrationality' to each other and the curious investigator. The complexity of an industrial economy is explained away instead of explained.

This is a theme to which we shall return towards the end of this section in relation to the abandoning of the informal economy approach as such. However, this tendency also appears elsewhere in Henry's work. His view of the hidden economy, developed further in conjunction with Mars (Henry and Mars, 1978), bestows on formal economic activity a greater regularity, order and logic than it in fact possesses, primarily, one suspects, in order to distinguish it from hidden economic activity. Many studies by industrial sociologists, however, have revealed the routinely informal and non-bureaucratic nature of many aspects of 'formal' work-places and institutional work organizations.

Two further criticisms of Henry's model may be summarized as follows. First, by concentrating on a set of illegal activities subsumed under the term 'hidden economy', he ignores the distinctions between types of activity when viewed from the actors' points of view. Providing a commodity for a member of one's own family, on the one hand, and for a casual acquaintance in a pub, on the other, are equivalent in Henry's model; this may not be so in the eyes of the participants. A distinction between the meanings attached to behaviour is crucial in an approach which, like Henry's, concentrates on the values and cultural models underlying behaviour. Second, the relationship between different kinds of economic activity is obscured in the separate economy model. Economic spheres are not defined in terms of independent criteria: 'They are separate spheres because they are distinct and they are distinct because they are separate spheres' (Jenkins, 1982:6). The resultant model is, at best, tautological, and, at worst, obfuscatory.

What is clear, however, in the work of Ditton, Henry and Mars, is that 'hidden' economic activity is dependent upon formal employment. What is not clear is why it should be described as belonging to a different economic sphere just because it is illegal. We shall move on to consider other forms of economic activity that have been described as 'underground' to see if the rationale behind this classification can be made any clearer.

Prominence was given in Chapter 3 to the classification of separate economies developed by Ferman and Berndt (1981), arising out of their study of Detroit households (Ferman *et al.*, 1978). Their study clearly indicates some of the benefits to be gained from an informal economy approach. Their basic model and major findings have already been summarized. Here we wish to deal specifically with what they have to say concerning the interdependence of the regular and irregular economies (Ferman and Berndt, 1981:32–7), the latter term encompassing Henry's hidden economy.

Their observations concerning this relationship are twofold. First, the irregular economy is seen to serve basic functions with respect to the regular economy. Secondly, the structure of society is believed to influence the form and content of irregular economic activity. The relationship is not presented, however, as one of dominance and subordination. The irregular economy is not merely the outcome of economic recession, but is the consequence of an economic and social structure which is dependent on it. For those living in the ghetto, the irregular economy may be a survival mechanism, but for those living in the middle-class suburb it is a means of obtaining goods and services that are difficult to obtain or are too highly priced in the regular market. Despite the crude functionalism sometimes evident in their approach, Ferman and Berndt do provide a comprehensive catalogue of the myriad connections between formal and that part of informal production, irregular economic production, which is quantifiable in monetary terms.

The Detroit study identified four functions which the irregular economy performs for the regular economy. First, the irregular economy consumes goods produced in the regular economy. The raw materials used to produce goods in the irregular economy are, for the most part, obtained through regular sources. Second, the irregular economy serves as a means of distribution of regularly produced goods. It does this in a number of ways. Regular products are transformed into new goods sold in the regular economy. These are the raw materials mentioned above. Goods originally produced and sold in the regular economy are recirculated in the irregular economy, for example items sold in garage or jumble sales. Goods purchased or stolen from regular sources are sold irregularly, such as items bought from door-to-door vendors who do not declare their income. Products obtained from regular sources are used to provide services irregularly, as in the case of the 'off the books' plumber or builder. Third, the irregular economy maintains products produced in the regular economy. The repair of appliances through the regular economy may be more expensive than their replacement through regular means. In such cases, maintenance by irregular means is a cheaper alternative. Finally, the irregular economy produces goods and services that are distributed through the regular economy. The out-worker in the clothing industry produces goods for an employer who sells in the regular market. The worker is not a regular employee protected by employment regulations and paying tax.

There are three major ways – economic, political and social – in which the institutional patterns of society shape the irregular economy as defined by Ferman and Berndt. These would appear to be the changes in conditions which stimulate the small transformations (to use Gershuny's term) between different economic 'spheres'.

To look at the economic dimension first, the demand for irregular goods and services, and the supply of workers to the irregular economy, is affected by conditions pertaining in the regular economy and its markets. Demand may be a function of the availability, distribution, supply and value of goods or services in the regular economy. For example, marijuana and heroin are not available through the regular economy. On another tack, 'ethnic' goods may not have a sufficiently large market to make their regular provision profitable. More precisely, the poor reward offered for certain services, such as baby-sitting, in the regular economy, may restrict their supply. Generally speaking, broad changes in the economic climate, of either expansion or recession, may make the use of regular sources more or less attractive in the fulfilment of perceived needs. Where a market is not catered for, or is inadequately catered for, by regular means, then it may find fulfilment through irregular provision.

A number of economic factors also affect the supply of workers to the irregular economy. More people may seek irregular work at a time of recession. The population of small businesses tends to increase during times of high unemployment. Self-employment in the irregular economy may be an attractive alternative to no work at all. Conversely, an expansion in the regular economy may see a movement of workers from irregular to regular employment, although an increased demand for certain irregular services at a time of economic expansion is also a possibility. These observations are broadly in keeping with Cassel's view that the shadow economy 'is booming whenever the offical economy reveals secular stagnation symptoms and vice versa' (1983:12).

People may choose to participate in the irregular economy for a variety of reasons, some economic, others not, but usually for a combination of these. No other work may be available to them. Irregular work may appear more lucrative to them than regular employment. It may supplement regular income, avoid the costs of regular enterprise in the form of book-keeping requirements and social security payments, or allow for the avoidance of taxation. Non-economic benefits include freedom, autonomy, and flexibility in the work situation. But perhaps most significant of all, Ferman and Berndt point out that in particular social contexts there may well be more opportunities for irregular rather than regular employment, and this obviously encourages participation. Ferman and Berndt exhibit a greater degree of understanding of the variety of motivations of individuals than does Gershuny in his discussion of opportunity costs and household self-provisioning.

This wide range of economic factors sets the limits within which people 'choose' to work. In some cases, they may choose to work in the irregular economy. In other cases, they are forced to do so because of the lack of any alternative. We have noted, in Chapter 3, Pahl's early view that participation in the informal economy could provide an attractive alternative to work in the formal sphere. He has since modified his views on this subject, but in response to the original idea it has been argued that participation in informal economic activity usually offers an inferior work situation to that of the formal sphere (Pinnaro and Pugliese, 1985). Under such circumstances there may be social resistance to the conditions of work and livelihood in the informal sector.

The second set of factors is rooted in the political sphere. Political factors actually define irregularity through licensing, regulation and tax and criminal laws. It is the political apparatus of the state which manages economic exchanges, and in so doing creates regularity and irregularity. Rules and regulations are drawn up to encourage economic development, to protect employees and consumers and to fund the public provision of services by the state. Certain goods and services are outlawed on social and moral grounds. However, most irregular economic activity is not, as a practice in itself, illegal. Rather, the circumstances within which it is practised render it illegal. It is the non-declaration of earnings to avoid taxation or loss of welfare payments, rather than the activity itself, that is illegal in many cases. Government regulation actually stimulates irregular economic activity in some ways, particularly in relation to its income support and taxation policies. The keeping of accurate records by small businesses for taxation purposes may mean unprofitability and hence inaccurate records are kept, thus consigning that proportion of its business which is unaccounted for to the irregular economy. Similarly, the declaration of additional earnings from a second job may entail the disappearance of any appreciable marginal economic gain as a result of a changed position as regards taxation bands. Entitlement to social security benefit may also be jeopardized if part-time earnings are declared. Declaration of these kinds of activity is, understandably, not forthcoming and they are therefore designated a part of the irregular economy. To use another example, restrictive licensing policies might bar qualified persons from practising their occupation regularly or legitimately. They practise on an irregular basis instead. Others may not even be aware that they are undertaking an activity which contravenes regulations. Intent is not a requirement of irregularity or informality.

The influence of political factors in encouraging informal activity has been much debated. This is particularly so with respect to the relationship between taxation and the extent of informal economic activity. This topic will be dealt with further in detail in Chapter 5, with respect to indirect methodologies for measuring the size of the informal economy. Here, we must simply mention the relationship which has been posited by some commentators between levels of social security benefits and participation in informal economic activity. The Detroit study does not go into this in detail, but Ferman and Berndt do suggest the loss of social security entitlement as a reason for keeping part-time earnings undeclared and therefore consigning such part-time activity to the irregular economy.

United Kingdom society experiences periodic minor 'moral panics' about so-called 'welfare scroungers' (Golding and Middleton, 1978; 1982). Public concern about the numbers of those on supplementary benefit who are earning more than the statutory maximum allowance a week without declaring it appears on occasions to reach a level out of all proportion to the cost to the state which is likely to be involved. Smith's demonstration that the United Kingdom government spends more on the enforcement of social security benefit regulations, per pound recovered, than on the detection of tax evasion is telling (1986:74). In addition, those caught engaging in benefit fraud are more likely to be prosecuted than those evading taxes. Pahl (1984) has shown that on the Isle of Sheppey the unemployed, those most likely to be on supplementary benefit, are in fact much the least likely to be engaging in informal economic activity. In Hartlepool, in the north-east of England, diminished access to informal economic activities is one aspect of the increasing polarization between the employed and the unemployed (Morris, 1987). The same appears to be the case in West Germany (Smith and Wied-Nebbeling, 1986:49–64). Mingione (1985), writing of urban areas in Southern Italy, finds that state allowances, rather than encouraging people to engage in 'off the books' activity, are an indispensable complement to the very low incomes derived from the occasional and informal economic activities which may be all that are available. Ferman and Berndt's observations as to the effect of levels of social security payment clearly need to be applied carefully, as their general application can lead to misconceptions which may have dire consequences for those thought to be engaging in informal economic activity.

The third set of factors to which Ferman and Berndt refer, in addition to the economic and political factors mentioned already, might be termed 'social' factors. Here they are concerned, first, with the sources of the networks which exist between producers and consumers of goods and services in the irregular economy, and second, the sources of the norms and values which influence participation in irregular economic activity.

While irregular economic activity takes place outside state legislation and regulation, it is not without its structure or pattern. Expectations exist which condition informal economic activity, whether it be the highly organized crime syndicate or co-operation between neighbours: 'Threats and sanctions are communicated through informal networks and are well understood by the community of participants' (Ferman and Berndt, 1981:37). A great deal of irregular economic activity is dependent upon the propinquity of prior association and membership of social networks. Consumer protection is assured, not by written guarantee, but in terms of reputation among participants.

The dependence upon already established networks for

participation in informal economic activity has been convincingly documented. It is one of the most common results of recent research into the informal economy. Edgell and Hart, for example, established that over two-thirds of the firemen in their sample found out about informal economic opportunities, at least in part, from inside contacts at work: 'Thus being part of the Fire Service strongly influences one's social network which in turn affects one's knowledge of, and opportunity to undertake, informal work' (Edgell and Hart, 1988:31–2). A factor contributing therefore to the relatively low likelihood that the unemployed will participate in informal economic activity, which has been noted in Pahl's work (1984; 1988) and elsewhere, is their lack of the social networks provided by a formal job situation. Hence the hypothesis that a decline in labour intensive industry might lead to a shrinkage in the informal economy. Harris *et al.* (1985) report that the opportunities for obtaining short fixed-term jobs and access to informal economic activity among those made redundant in South Wales were affected by the degree of development of local social networks. Highly developed social networks increase the range of opportunities. It appears to be the case that, in this respect, being in formal employment will actually *increase* the likelihood of engaging in informal economic activity. Further confirmation of this conclusion comes from Morris's research in Hartlepool (1987).

The organization of self-help: communal economic activity

One 'economy' remains to be discussed in terms of Gershuny's (1983) model, the communal economy. Again, he does not discuss this economy in as great detail as the household economy, but he does make some observations concerning its relationship to the formal economy. Gershuny argues that the movement of productive activity from the formal to the communal sphere will become increasingly important. Handy also points out that the opportunities for work in the communal sphere are potentially great, although their development or facilitation by government may be required (1982:12).

Gershuny notes that the public-sector provision of services is labour intensive. Seventy to eighty per cent of the cost of public services is accounted for by the salaries of public employees (1983:40). Calls for increased spending by the state on public services, on the one hand, have to be balanced politically against calls for a reduction in public spending, on the other. Gershuny offers, in the communal sector, a possible resolution of this conflict of interest, a way of increasing public provision while decreasing, or at least not necessarily increasing, public expenditure. Public spending could be reduced by a transfer of service activities, such as the care of the young and the old, back to the communal economy. The state could provide the material equipment and infrastructure for use by community groups, thus helping to reduce the largest part of its expenditure, the wages and salaries bill.

The point is illustrated with reference to the provision of crèche facilities by local government. While acknowledging that such provision is currently meagre in the United Kingdom, Gershuny points out that expenditure on this public service tends to be in keeping with expenditure on public services generally, in that 70 per cent is labour cost, and 30 per cent is capital equipment cost (1983:171). Such crèche facilities are fully staffed. Gershuny suggests a change to a situation of mixed labour: on the one hand paid professionals (providing technical, advisory and organizational skills), and, on the other, volunteers (parents). Such a policy innovation might lead to a change in the pattern of expenditure to 70 per cent on capital equipment and 30 per cent on paid labour. Gershuny calculates that, on this basis, two and a half times as many crèche facilities could be offered for the same level of public expenditure.

These innovations are likely, of course, to meet opposition from certain interest groups, for example trades unions, but Gershuny feels that they need not automatically result in a drop in formal employment. He suggests that the increased efficiency of the provision of such services would encourage a local authority, acting rationally, to transfer expenditure into this sphere of provision. By doubling its expenditure, for example, it could increase the provision of crèche services five-fold.

Moving from the particular to the general, Gershuny suggests that an increase in the productivity of all public services would encourage households, again acting rationally by his lights, to transfer expenditure from disposable income to their taxes to pay for such services. Just as demand for services may be expected to decrease with rising prices, so the fall of effective real prices as a result of increased productivity might be expected to lead to an increase in public expenditure because of increased demand. Gershuny argues that this applies to other public services, such as the university and medical sectors. A reduction in variable costs, such as labour, and an increase in fixed or capital costs will, ideally, increase productivity.

It is in relation to communal economic activity that transformations are most clearly dependent upon state intervention. The short-term advantages to government of this kind of development might appear to be attractive. However, yet again Gershuny is applying a narrow definition of rationality in suggesting that citizens would be prepared to pay higher taxes, and local authorities to increase their public expenditure, in the light of increased productivity in certain spheres. Gershuny does not take into account either cultural constraints (such as a reluctance to pay tax) or political constraints (such as effective cuts in local authority budgets) which affect the situation.

It is worth at this point emphasizing the context within which the possibility of the movement of activities from the formal to the informal economies has been canvassed. Informal economic activity has only been treated seriously by governments since the onset of economic recession.

This fact has not gone unnoticed by social scientists and much recent work has focused upon this area. The issue of informal care provision within the context of communal social networks, as an alternative to formal, state-organized provision, has become bound up in the United Kingdom and elsewhere with the policy goal of de-institutionalizing much social service provision, both as a desirable end in itself and as a means of saving money (Bulmer, 1987; Willmott, 1986).

Gershuny, however, does not discuss the practical question of who will support the voluntary labour required in his model. Presumably this links in with his notion of the opportunity cost to households. Communal production, by this token, becomes part of a household's work strategy. We are then faced with a possible (or likely) situation in which certain households and communities will have members who engage in communal production while others do not. This is the clear implication of the programme of research into neighbouring relations and informal care which the late Philip Abrams left unfinished on his death in 1981 (Bulmer, 1986). For Handy (1984), this would merely be an extension of an already well-established pattern and tradition of voluntary work in the United Kingdom and elsewhere. Once again, no account is taken of the differences which exist between groups or sections of society in their ability or inclination to engage in voluntary work, or of the social and political implications of polarization in the communal economy.

Doubts and scepticism: criticisms of the informal economy model

To reiterate, the informal economy has been seen as a liberating alternative to work (Pahl, 1980), a reservoir where the unused demand for labour is stored (Handy, 1984) and, as we have just seen, a means whereby government can reduce public expenditure on social welfare (Gershuny, 1983). Connolly notes that the economic and political context which normally gives rise to the use of the informal economy concept in theorizing is characterized by: 'empty public treasuries facing increasing demands for social expenditure, unemployment, economic recession and the emergence of austerity policies' (1985:58). Policy measures are consequently formulated on the basis of assumptions that national growth rates are under-estimated (because they are calculated on the basis of formal economic figures), that the unemployment statistics are exaggerated (because many of those claiming unemployment benefit are in fact engaged in remunerative work), that formal employment is restricted by legislation and collective agreements with trades unions (whereas informal employment is more flexible and beset with none of these burdens), that the inflation index is over-estimated (because prices in the informal sector tend to be lower than those in the formal sector) and that taxes are too high (with the consequence that many activities are pushed into the underground economy). The informal economy is invariably seen as operating to the detriment of the formal economy and in favour of individuals who participate in informal economic activity. This model of the situation may be summarized thus: 'the informal sector is employment disguised as unemployment' (Connolly, 1985:62). The policy consequences of taking such a view include, *inter alia*, increased deregulation and lower taxation.

It is perhaps a reflection on the lack of cross fertilization of ideas that the debate over the informal economy in the industrialized world should have attracted so much political and academic interest at a time when its influence in the study of Third World societies was already in decline. This international interest in the application of this model to the 'developed' world continues (Ferman *et al.*, 1987; Gaertner and Wenig, 1985; Grazia, 1984; Rose, 1985; Smith, 1986; Smith and Wied-Nebbeling, 1986; Thomas, 1988; Weiss, 1987). The critique of the informal economies model emanating from development studies is extensive and will not be reviewed in full. Others (e.g. Bryant, 1982) have reviewed the debate more effectively than time or space will allow us here and extensive reference is made to this literature in the volume edited by Redclift and Mingione (1985). Roldan, in that volume, summarizes an important line of argument which is as applicable to the industrialized world as it is to developing countries. In this view, the informal sector approach is seen to suffer from four basic deficiencies. We shall deal with these in turn.

Roldan points out that the informal sector concept offers a descriptive framework within which to place occupational categories (1985:249). In Chapter 3 we reviewed some of the large number of terms which had been used to describe various sorts of activity. The descriptive rather than explanatory nature of these classifications was brought out most clearly in relation to the colour coding of various so-called economies. It is this lack of rigorous *explanatory* value that is the 'informal economy' model's first major deficiency.

The second shortcoming involves the basic dualism inherent in the informal economy model which, as Jenkins (1982) and others have pointed out, over-simplifies the relationship between different economic activities. The formal/informal classification is simplistic and the labelling of all economic activities as either one or the other ignores more subtle differences between intermediate economic activities. The inconsistencies in Handy's (1984) colour classification can in part be attributed to this problem. At one point the 'burgeoning personal services and home businesses' which he describes are allocated to the black economy (1984:18), while elsewhere in the same text (1984:42) they have become a part of the mauve economy, 'on the fringe of the formal economy'. Handy also recognizes the potential for such activities to move out of the informal economy altogether and become proper businesses (1984:48).

The third problem which Roldan identifies has also been alluded to in the work of Jenkins (1982). The informal sector concept offers no specific positive criteria according to which an activity can be assigned to one economy or another. Activities in one economy are defined by their *lack* of the characteristics possessed by activities in the other economy. The formal and informal sectors are viewed as autonomous, whereas, for Roldan, their relationship is one of domination and subordination. There is a strong tendency in the writing of Gershuny for example, to emphasize the *choice* open to individuals or household units at the expense of giving adequate recognition to the constraints under which they operate. Although greater consideration is given to structural effects in the work of Ferman and Berndt, for example, they do not give primacy to these over human agency and choice.

The final deficiency outlined by Roldan refers to the effects of conceptualizing economic activities in terms of homogeneous 'separate economies'. Theorizing economic activities in this way leads to the formulation of generalized and undifferentiated policies which generally act to the detriment of those participating in local informal activities, whose circumstances and behaviour will be extremely heterogeneous. We have already speculated about the adverse effect that national action concerned with the relationship between the non-declaration of earnings and eligibility for social security benefits might have for those involved. Of course, not all those claiming social security benefits are omitting to declare remunerative employment. In fact, as discussed earlier, much research has shown that those claiming social security benefits are less likely to be engaged in non-declared economic activity than those in full-time formal employment. Those undertaking informal work are doing so for a variety of reasons and have a variety of interests which are neither identical nor necessarily complementary.

Some interesting arguments which are of relevance to this highly critical evaluation of the informal economy model have been offered by Gershuny himself. He suggests that, 'the informal economy is of course not really an economy in itself but rather the neglected part of the full economic system which includes both formal and informal production' (1983:32). He says elsewhere that, 'the informal economy...is of course not a separate economy at all but an integral part of the system by which work, paid and unpaid, satisfies human needs' (1985:129). In his more recent work he has been concerned with productive systems and their interrelationships rather than distinct economies (1983). This notwithstanding, however, his model and the relationship between the parts remain largely the same and he continues to talk about work 'outside' the formal economy (Gershuny and Miles, 1985:34).

Pahl has accepted some responsibility for the confusion surrounding the informal economy model as applied to the United Kingdom and other market economies of the industrialized world (1984:117). Gershuny and Pahl originally adopted the term 'informal economy' to distinguish between different patterns of the provision of services. In retrospect, Pahl accepts that some other terminology might have been more appropriate, terminology which would have made it clear that they were referring to spheres of service provision. It is necessary to emphasize at this point that our criticism of Pahl and Gershuny's use of the informal economy model should not obscure the important contribution which they have made, separately and together, to the identification and analysis of some of the processes which characterize contemporary United Kingdom society, in particular with respect to the changing mode of provision of economic services. Modes of service provision affect the range of tasks undertaken by households as a means of 'getting by'. Household work patterns provide a tracer for wider political and economic changes and tendencies. Pahl, for example, identifies different sources of labour (self-provided, informal/communal, formal) which are important to household work strategies. Households use their own labour in distinctive ways and draw on labour from outside the household where necessary. All forms of work and sources of labour must be explored within the specific arenas in which they arise, in the context of situationally determined divisions of labour. For the moment, we leave aside the question of sources of labour (we shall deal with it specifically in Chapter 7) in order to conclude this section with a model of our own devising within which to conceptualize forms of economic activity.

Work and employment: an alternative analytical framework

The basis of this framework was laid in Chapter 2, with our

discussion of the meanings of work and our distinction, within an overall category of economic activity, between work and employment. We suggested that employment involves working for someone else. Although the distinction between work and employment is apparently clear-cut, there are, however, situations in which this distinction may be blurred. Recognizing this, we wish to propose that work and employment, as contrasting ideal types of economic activity, be regarded as involving different relationships positioned at the opposite ends of a continuum of 'real life' situations. In addition, we wish to retain a distinction between informality and formality. These too, however, should be regarded as representing the poles of a continuum.

In this chapter and the last we have dwelt on these notions, of formality and informality, as they have been applied to different 'economies'. In explaining the use of this distinction in delineating the boundaries of these putative economies we have concluded that it is, at best, of limited usefulness. Our argument is basically similar to that which has become accepted by many organizational sociologists: at best, the sharp dichotomy between the formal and the informal is a myth (albeit one which organizational members can often manipulate for their own ends), at worst, it is a barrier to understanding. While rejecting the notion of different economies *per se*, however, we recognize the importance of retaining a distinction between formality and informality with reference to particular economic activities in specific social situations. While the distinction between types of economic activity cannot always be maintained on the basis of their being publicly recorded or regulated, the broad opposition between formality and informality is a useful aid in the analysis of such activities. Specific practices in specific contexts can, therefore, be placed according to their positions on two axes: between work and employment, on the one hand, and between formality and informality, on the other, as in the notional examples in Figure 1. In Chapter 7, we shall return to this framework and elaborate upon it using concrete examples.

This is the analytical framework within which we intend to proceed. While admittedly largely descriptive at one level, at another level its theoretical content is specified by an understanding of the nature of economic activity within capitalism, on the one hand, and a view of the historical development of

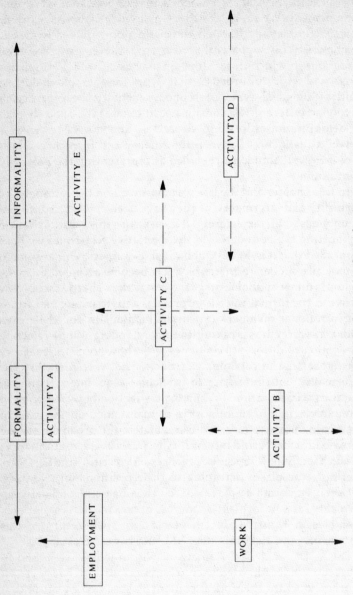

Figure 1 A model of formal and informal economic activity

bureaucratic organizations and the state, on the other. Activities can be related to one another within the framework in terms of their possession of more or less of any particular attribute. Some categories of activity, such as our imaginary examples B, C or D in Figure 1, may occupy indeterminate locations, depending on their context.

To reiterate, in this chapter we have critically discussed the work of Gershuny, Pahl, Henry, Ditton, Ferman and Berndt and others who have used and developed the informal economy model. Their specification of separate economic spheres has not, however, prevented them from determining points at which these discrete spheres intersect. In fact, there are so many intersections that those which are given prominence in particular studies appear to reflect more the concerns of the writer than the significance or ubiquity of the relationship. What is most questionable is whether the identification of 'economies' as formal or informal, regular or irregular, has any usefulness other than to draw attention to the fact that, while some economic activities are taken into account by the state in the compilation of annual accounts and statements, others are not. This is not to detract from the importance of such an observation; simply to suggest that a greater understanding might be gained by conceptualizing the range or pattern of economic activities in another way. Their conceptualization as inhabiting separate spheres or economies does, at best, little to enhance our understanding of the relationship between economic practices and forms. We have suggested a simple alternative framework within which it is possible to analyse various different kinds of economic activity. In the next two chapters we shall retain the informal economy model, however unsatisfactory, in our discussion of research methodologies, since it has been within this tradition that research problems and methods have largely been formulated.

Chapter 5

INDIRECT RESEARCH APPROACHES

In the previous chapter we discussed the proliferation of models of the hidden or informal economy. These were criticized strongly on a number of counts: for the *ad hoc* nature of their theorization, the inappropriateness of the 'separate economies' model to the complex, interconnected mixed economies under discussion, and their apparent inability to produce a coherent set of criteria with which to distinguish rigorously either the formal/public from the informal/hidden, or the various subterranean economies from each other. In this chapter and the following we shall discuss the methodological problems and inadequacies which are a consequence of these conceptual weaknesses.

There are two broad approaches to doing research into informal economic activity. *Direct* approaches involve the intensive investigation of samples – usually small samples – of the population by investigators whose specific purpose is to obtain information on informal economic activity. *Indirect* approaches concentrate upon the study of already available statistics, such as those contained in the Blue Books referred to by Davis (1985) in relation to the United Kingdom. Studies of this kind typically attempt to estimate the volume or value of informal economic activity in monetary terms (see also, Smith, 1987).

In this chapter we shall discuss indirect approaches. Mattera (1985:42) further sub-divides these into those 'which look at traces of underground economic activity in economic aggregates such as money supply', which we term, following Boyle

(1984:33), the 'monetary method', and those 'based on discrepancies between expenditure and income'. Thomas, in dealing
with what he terms the 'statistical fingerprints' of the black
economy, limits himself to an analysis of these two types of
indirect measures (1988:169). In addition, we shall look at
attempts to estimate the value of profit-oriented crime, studies
of labour force statistics, multi-variate analyses which take as
their starting point the rate of taxation, studies which suggest
that informal economic activity might in fact be shrinking, and,
finally, a study which has approached indirectly that area of
informal activity not normally subject to attempted measurement, the household.

Tracing hidden economic activity in the money supply

To look first at the monetary method, Henry, writing in 1976,
argued that the increasing demand for $50 and $100 notes in the
United States between 1960 and 1970, a period which saw a rapid
increase in non-cash methods of payment such as personal
cheque accounts and credit cards, could only be explained in
terms of an expansion in profit-oriented crime and tax evasion.
He argued that these activities required extra cash so as to avoid
leaving traceable records. By relating the demand for large
denomination notes ($50 and over) to factors such as price levels,
personal consumption expenditures and federal income tax
revenues, he calculated the extra demand for large denomination
notes that resulted from tax evasion to be as high as $30 billion
for the year 1973. Looking at organized crime, he used a variety
of factors to support his view that the 'value' of profit-motivated
crime amounted to a similar annual figure.

Henry was concerned to encourage the Federal government to
recall large denomination notes in order to undermine the
activities of tax evaders and large-scale criminal operators.
Mattera points out that he ignores the degree to which small-
scale operators, for example the skilled worker who 'moonlights',
contributed to the greater demand for cash. Mattera also notes
that Henry seemed unconcerned that his estimates of unreported
income amounted to 5 per cent of the official Gross National
Product or GNP (1985:44-5).

Boyle, applying this method to the Republic of Ireland, doubts
whether the significant increase in the number and proportion of

IR£20 and IR£50 notes in circulation can, in fact, be taken to signify an increase in economic activity in the 'black' sector (1984). He argues that price levels are a key variable affecting the mix of denominations in circulation. An increase in the use of large denomination notes is simply consistent with the public's attempts to cut down the quantity of small bills in its possession as a consequence of increased prices and inflation generally. He shows that while the average size of notes in circulation in the Irish economy doubled between 1960 and 1983, price levels increased almost ninefold.

Freud, however, does not see the increase in large denomination notes in the United Kingdom as the result of increased consumer spending and inflation. In his view, the 420 per cent increase of the aggregate value of £10 and £20 notes in circulation between 1972 and 1978 can only be explained in terms of increased informal economic activity. Consumer expenditure grew during this period by only 140 per cent. The increase results, it is argued, from a situation where, 'people tend to pay their "black" plumbing bills for, say, £100 in £10 and £20 notes, rather than in £1 or £5 notes' (Freud, 1979;16).

Macafee, by contrast, has urged caution in interpreting the increase in the number of large denomination banknotes in circulation in the United Kingdom as an indication of increased informal economic activity (Macafee, 1980). While there has undoubtedly been an increase which cannot be explained solely by inflation, Macafee suggests that there is in Britain a tradition of payment in cash. To advance the argument further, Tanzi (1982) observes that many informal transactions involve the smaller denomination notes which are in everyday use, as with baby-sitters or window cleaners, for example. What is more, covert transactions requiring the transfer of larger sums can easily be undertaken using false or second bank accounts. For both Macafee and Tanzi, therefore, the monetary method is an unreliable approach to the measurement of informal economic activity.

At the time Henry was writing, little attention was paid to his work. Governments were not concerned as yet with the possible scale of informal economic activity in their countries. For example, Heertje *et al.* record the disbelieving response of the Dutch Central Statistical Office to the first publication on the subject in Holland; it 'dismissed the suggestion that it should investigate the size of the unofficial economy' (1982:104). It was Gutmann's work which brought the phenomenon into the mainstream of public debate in the United States (1977). He estimated that the 'subterranean economy' amounted to some $176 billion in 1976. This estimation was based on the extra demand for currency created by those who had to carry out their illegitimate transactions in cash. Instead of looking at the amount of cash in circulation, Gutmann examined the composition of the money supply, that is the ratio of currency to current accounts.

Gutmann commenced his analysis by assuming that there was no subterranean economy in the United States prior to the Second World War. He argued that levels of taxation were so low as to make the need for tax evasion strategies unnecessary; as a consequence it is legitimate, he suggests, to take the ratio of currency to current accounts for this period as the baseline norm. He noted, first, that the ratio had risen substantially by the mid-1970s; second, that $29 billion was in circulation beyond the figure required for legitimate transactions, assuming that subterranean cash circulated at the same rate as 'legitimate money stock'; and, third, that the subterranean GNP amounted to more than 10 per cent of the officially calculated national income.

Smith has noted that Gutmann's method, if applied to the United Kingdom, would seem to suggest that the 'black economy' – everything from crime to tax evasion and benefit fraud – has actually shrunk in recent years. Using the slightly broader concept of 'private sector sight deposits', Smith calculates that the ratio of cash to such deposits remained steady during the 1960s and 1970s, declining sharply in the 1980s: 'Gutmann's method would therefore imply no change in the UK black economy during the 1960s and 1970s, and a decline in the level of underground activity during the 1980s' (Smith, 1986:98). While acknowledging the possibility of such a trend, Smith is sceptical about the usefulness of the method inasmuch as it ignores the variety of possible causal variables.

Gutmann's method was also applied to the Republic of Ireland by Boyle (1984). He found that from 1960 to 1969 the ratio of currency to current accounts fell, but between 1970 and 1975 it increased dramatically. It declined again between 1976 and 1978 but has been rising steadily ever since. The overall trend has been one of an increasing ratio of currency to current accounts. Boyle does not, however, see this as conclusive evidence of an increase in 'black' economic activity. Many other factors must also be taken into consideration. He suggests that the stock of current accounts is actually a poor indicator of the use of such accounts. Such data only refer, for example, to current accounts that are in credit and ignore overdrafts. Inflation promotes the transfer of holdings to interest-bearing assets by both currency and current account holders, and though the direction in response to interest rate changes may be similar for the two groups, the relative size of the response may be quite different. Current account stock can be switched much more quickly than a similar stock of currency. This may provide an explanation for the increased ratio of currency to current accounts in recent years.

Mattera (1985) echoes these criticisms: Gutmann failed to take account of factors, other than those to do with the subterranean economy, which might have contributed to the decline in the currency ratio. Boyle, for example, suggests that the 1970 Irish banking industrial dispute, which distorted the money statistics, could partly account for the dramatic increase between 1969 and 1971 in Ireland. Mattera further suggests that the fact that related ratios, such as that between currency and the GNP, showed no consistent signs of increase in the United States during the period he was examining casts doubt upon Gutmann's findings. Boyle concludes that, 'this methodology is so fraught with ambiguities and laced with at best speculative assumptions that the method could not be used with confidence' (1984:37).

Thomas (1988:179–80) highlights the problems associated with the need to locate a year when the black economy did not exist. Gutmann's assumption that there was no black economy in the United States prior to the Second World War seems to Thomas *ad hoc* and determined by the availability of data rather than any other factor. Indeed, Smithies' work on the history of the black economy in England (1984) lends support to the idea that some black economic activity has been a feature of developed economies throughout the twentieth century. A method which measures the black economy from a time when it is believed not to have existed is suspect on these grounds if no other.

Some attempt has been made to take into consideration factors outside the hidden economy: Tanzi (1980) in the United States and Matthews (1983) and Matthews and Rastogi (1985) in the United Kingdom, for example. Rather than attributing the entire increase in the cash to current accounts ratio to greater levels of informal economic activity, such approaches focus upon only that proportion of the increase which can be shown to be the result of changes in the presumed determinants of informal economic activity. A distinction is therefore made between the formal and informal economic variables which are likely to affect the ratio of cash to current accounts.

The work of Matthews, referred to above, may be used as an exemplar. He takes account of three possible determinants of the hidden economy in the United Kingdom: one, the rate of employer's National Insurance contributions; two, the average income tax rate for a married man with two children; and three, an estimation of the level of Unemployment Benefit and other welfare payments. Matthews incorporates these variables into a cash to current accounts ratio equation, in order to estimate the size of the United Kingdom 'subterranean economy'. He estimates that between 1972 and 1974, this fell from 5.5 per cent to 2.3 per cent of the Gross Domestic Product (GDP), rising to 7.8 per cent of GDP in 1978, 12.1 per cent in 1980 and 15.9 per cent in 1983. From these findings, Matthews infers that a major proportion of the registered unemployed population – about 1.3 million out of 3 million – are actually 'employed' in the subterranean economy. The official unemployment statistics are, therefore, highly inflated.

Matthews' approach is more sophisticated than Gutmann's. It is not, however, without its critics. Smith, for example, points out (1986:100) that Matthews interprets the level of transactions in the black economy as solely a function of tax and benefit rates. Other considerations, such as the penalties and risks attached to detection, which are likely to affect decisions to engage in informal economic activity are not taken into account. Smith admits, however, that difficulties in quantifying such 'subjective' variables may have influenced their omission.

Smith's critique extends (1986:101) to questioning the appropriateness and value of the statistical variables which Matthews employs. Without wishing to adumbrate his argument in detail here, suffice it to say that he casts considerable doubt upon the utility of the variables used both by Matthews (1983) and by Matthews and Rastogi in their later formulation (1985) of the relationship between the demand for cash and the size of the hidden economy. With regard to the latter study, Smith further questions the validity of the authors' identification of a causal relationship between rises in unemployment levels and the growth of the black economy; even using Matthews and Rastogi's own figures, 'the black economy has expanded most at a time when unemployment rose comparatively little' (Smith, 1986:106). Thomas draws attention to 'some interesting differences between the results obtained in the two studies involving Matthews' (1988:175). All the predictions made by Matthews (1983) fall well below those of Matthews and Rastogi (1985) but the latter study makes nothing more than a cursory reference to the earlier one and does not address the question of these differences.

Later in this chapter we will discuss other attempts to quantify the hidden economy by estimating the size of the unregistered labour force. For the moment, suffice it to say that those working in the footsteps of Gutmann have been unable to exorcise the investigation of cash to current accounts ratios of its severe – and, in our view, inherent – shortcomings. What Gutmann did achieve, however, was media exposure. His lasting contribution to the field is the stimulation of research in the area of indirect measurement techniques, including both refinements to the currency equation and macro-economic speculation, and the focusing of public attention on the phenomenon of unreported income.

The work of Feige (1981) provides us with a bridge between the putative measurement of the underground economy in the United States and attempts, mainly in the 1970s, to measure the size of the underground economy in the United Kingdom. Feige's figure for the size of the 'underground' economy in the United States was $700 billion, a figure amounting to nearly 27 per cent of the official GNP. He based his analysis on an estimate of the total transactions in the economy, taking into account such factors as the physical composition of paper money. He later applied this technique to the United Kingdom where he estimated the 'underground' economy to amount to 15 per cent of the GDP. Feige adopted as a simplifying assumption the notion that the relationship between the volume of non-financial transactions and the income produced by them is relatively stable. He argued that the total of non-financial transactions in the economy included monetary transactions in both the observed and the unobserved sectors, and that from them could be determined the total income that should have produced all these transactions. By subtracting the observed total from the estimated total, he claimed to have estimated the size of the informal economy. Feige's figures for non-financial transactions were obtained by examining the stock of currency in circulation, its velocity and measures of the volume of cheque transactions for financial purposes. On this basis he estimated that the unobserved economy in the United Kingdom was worth £28 billion, that it had grown during the 1970s, and that, if anything, this estimate was on the conservative side (1981: 210).

Boyle's (1984) estimate of the size of the black economy in Ireland using the monetary method is less ambiguous. Using mathematical forecasting techniques, he attempts to estimate the relationship between currency holdings and variables such as GDP, the price level and deposit interest rates, for a period when the black economy was judged not to be growing. Currency holdings are then forecast, using this mathematical relationship, for a period when the black economy is thought to be emergent. By multiplying the currency figure by the officially measured income velocity of circulation, an income figure is forthcoming. The size of the black economy in Ireland for the period 1975–83 is put, on this basis, at about 6 per cent of GDP and its increase in the late 1970s is seen to coincide vaguely with the increased taxation burden. Boyle does not claim that this method 'proves' that the black economy is the cause of the difference between actual and predicted currency holdings, it merely 'asserts' that it might be the cause.

Boyle argues that Feige's approach has advantages over the currency to current account ratio method. While the estimate of the component of the GDP produced by the black economy involves a deduction of the value of final transactions from the value of total transactions, just as the difference between the computed level of currency and the actual level of currency was used to estimate its size by Gutmann, Feige's approach allows cheques as well as cash to be included as a medium of exchange. Boyle acknowledges the problems with this approach which are identified by Mattera, namely that Feige's approach, as also the methods of Henry and Gutmann, relies on assumptions about the rate of circulation of money. Boyle points out that data can be obtained on transactions involving current accounts through the analysis of bank debit records. However, he acknowledges that data on currency turnover is much more problematic: 'There are no data whatsoever available for currency transactions' (1984:39). Boyle does provide a rough estimate for Ireland by postulating the number of transactions which can be performed during a unit of currency's lifetime and dividing this by the average life of that unit of currency. To obtain a further estimate of the total currency transactions, the resultant figure is multiplied by the stock of currency in circulation. The average life of a unit of currency may be estimated by dividing the stock of currency in circulation in a particular period by the number of notes destroyed during this period.

Boyle estimates that currency turnover in the Republic of Ireland increased by about 16 per cent between 1960 and 1969 and about 22 per cent between 1970 and 1980. Current account turnover increased by 24 per cent between 1960 and 1969 and by 162 per cent between 1970 and 1980. Boyle acknowledges, however, that there is no real way of knowing the absolute amount of transactions which a unit of currency can effect in a lifetime. On the basis of these assumptions, changes in the ratio of currency to current account turnover would indicate a movement in the value of the black economy.

Three major deficiencies in this method are identified by Boyle. First, only transactions where money is actually exchanged for goods or services should be included in the calculations. Other purely financial transactions which, however, are also included, such as the exchange of coin or cash withdrawals from current accounts, will serve to distort the measure of current account to cash turnover. Second, the method assumes a constancy in the average number of transactions of a unit of currency over time. Boyle suggests that no account is taken of technological changes in the production of bank notes, which might affect their quantity and hence the duration of their life-time. Finally, the fact that, according to these calculations, the black economy is equivalent to 27 per cent of GNP in the United States and 15 per cent of the GDP in the United Kingdom casts considerable doubt on the validity of this method. Boyle argues that these figures are unrealistically high. At best, this is merely the identification of a trend in the ratio of computed total transactions to offically measured transactions. Such 'method-ologies cannot provide conclusive answers, nor can they provide results with margins of error useful for decision-making' (Boyle, 1984:42).

Comparing income and expenditure

Attempts to measure the size of the informal economy in the United Kingdom using indirect methods have generally followed a different course to those of the American and Irish studies mentioned here. The underlying assumption of the income/ expenditure discrepancy approach has been that while people may attempt to conceal their true income, they will not conceal their true expenditure when interviewed in government surveys. It has long been the practice of the Central Statistical Office in the United Kingdom to adjust the preliminary GDP figures on the basis of the difference between the sum total of reported income and the invariably higher amount of reported expenditure. This practice was not made public by the CSO until the controversy surrounding the underground economy emerged in the late 1970s.

Macafee's (1980) CSO study revealed, for example, that in 1978 adjustments totalling £3640 million were included in the GDP statistics. Of this total, £2760 million (76 per cent) was for unreported self-employment income. In addition, he acknowledged that the CSO recognized that an additional amount of hidden activity was embodied within concealed expenditure (such as for illegal drugs) and concealed income in kind (fiddling). While the CSO could not make adjustments for the former, it did make a further small adjustment for the latter. This emphasis upon loss of revenue from the self-employed is supported by the remarks of the General Secretary of the Inland Revenue Staff Federation, who said in 1976 that,

> the low incomes to which the self-employed admit defy belief. Only 70,000 of them declare the average wage of £60 or more. Only 250,000 of them admit to more than £30 a week (quoted in O'Higgins, 1980:23).

For Macafee, then, incomes not declared for tax purposes were the largest part of the informal economy, amounting to 3.5 per cent of the GDP.

Dilnot and Morris, using the income/expenditure discrepancy method, came to similar conclusions about the size of the informal economy (1981). They claimed that it amounted to between £3000 and £4000 million, about 3 per cent of United Kingdom GDP. They reached this figure by examining, in detail, the spending patterns of 1000 out of the 7200 households in the Family Expenditure Survey. Households were found to have discrepancies of about £30 per week, on average, between their reported expenditure (taking account of legitimate factors such as pensioners using savings for current expenses) and their reported income.

The income/expenditure discrepancy approach has also been developed by Smith (1986:144) as the 'expenditure equations approach', differentiating between groups in terms of the incomes/expenditure relationship. He argues that certain sections of the population are better placed than others to conceal a component of their incomes. As an example, he cites self-employed painters and decorators compared to civil servants. Dilnot and Morris, cited above, also identify the self-employed as most likely to have hidden incomes, as do Smith and Wied-Nebbeling in their comparison of Britain and West Germany (1986). By comparing the reported spending behaviour of potential tax-evading populations – such as the self-employed – with that of a population matched for level of reported income but putatively less able to conceal income, significant differences in spending on particular goods may emerge. For example, the self-employed may spend more on foreign holidays than do employees at the same level of reported income. The more affluent consumption patterns of such supposed tax-evading populations may generate enough information to allow one to estimate their 'true' incomes. Using the 1982 Family Expenditure Survey, Smith estimates that the self-employed understate their income by between 10 and 20 per cent, as compared with Dilnot and Morris's estimate for all sections of the United Kingdom population of a 10 to 15 per cent understatement. Smith interprets his estimate as broadly commensurate with the understatement level assumed in the United Kingdom's national accounts (1986:153).

Mattera argues that the reported income/reported expenditure discrepancy measures are more convincing than the currency-based techniques, inasmuch as they are related to more solid data (expenditure figures) than the latter's dependence upon rates of circulation of money. However, estimates such as those made by Dilnot and Morris are dependent upon the accurate declaration of expenditure to government interviewers by respondents. Mattera suggests that it is somewhat naive to assume that people will not realize that a discrepancy between levels of income and levels of expenditure might be discerned as a result of the responses. He doubts that the small adjustments made to the GDP by the CSO to account for concealed expenditure and concealed income in kind 'begin to approximate to what is...being hidden' (Mattera, 1985:48). Equally convincing, however, is the criticism that, for most people, expenditure is more easily overestimated during a survey – inasmuch as records of spending are kept by few members of the population – than income, which, for employees, comes in regular, recorded, and often uniform instalments. If this criticism is valid, the CSO's adjustments are likely to overestimate levels of informal economic activity, rather than the reverse. O'Higgins (1980), using Macafee's figures, provides estimates of unrecorded income which come to not less than 5 per cent of the GDP, but he reaches no firm conclusions, stating that estimates of the size of the hidden economy are more a matter of faith than of hard fact. This is a harsh judgement, perhaps, but one with which the present authors are in agreement.

There are, therefore, widely different estimates of the size of the underground economy in both the United States and the United Kingdom, calculated using monetary and income/expenditure discrepancy method. Yet another attempt at indirect measurement, which we will not discuss in detail here, uses small business activity as a proxy for informal economic activity (Portes and Sassen-Koob, 1987). This method shares the shortcomings of the indirect approaches to the measurement of informal economic activity which we have identified above. There is a general consensus among researchers using indirect measurement approaches that government assumptions about the size of underground economic activity, in the absence of research, have been underestimates. Whether or not this consensus is justified by either the evidence or the rigour of the arguments is debatable. We turn now to look at a variety of other indirect methods which have been used to measure the approximate extent of underground economic activity.

Alternative approaches to indirect measurement

When discussing income which is in some sense stigmatized as 'illegal', it is important to recognize the distinction between perfectly respectable occupations, the income from which is illegal only because it is not declared for welfare or taxation purposes, and activities which, according to the law of the land, are illegal *per se* and the income from which is therefore not legitimate. Here we shall concentrate upon the latter but, as will become evident, the distinction between the two categories is not always easy to maintain when looking at specific situations.

Various attempts have been made to put a figure to illegal income, through analyses of the amount of cash in circulation as the result of criminal activities, as a result of the laundering of this money, and as a result of employee theft, cigarette smuggling and piracy. We will briefly deal with all these approaches.

In the United States, a report of the President's Commission on Law Enforcement (1967) estimated that as much as $7 billion profit was derived from illegal gambling, $350 million profit from the sale of drugs, $225 million from prostitution and $150 million from illegally produced alcohol. The validity of such figures must be seriously questioned, however. While the Commission was able to report with such apparent authority upon the value of criminal activities, it was unable to estimate the value of tax evasion and unreported income from legal sources. At the time of the Commission's work, interest in the value of criminal activity had long preceded any discussion of the underground economy as a whole. The same point can be made about tax evasion. Such phenomena were of interest to politicians and state bureaucracies both because they were seen to be a drain on the nation's resources, and as anti-social behaviour in a more straightforward sense.

A more systematic approach to the estimation of profit-oriented crime was attempted by the US Internal Revenue Service (IRS). Using original research undertaken in the 1970s, they estimated the unreported income which derived from three major criminal industries: illegal drugs, illegal gambling and female prostitution. The political reaction to their estimates provides interesting reading. Mattera (1985:57) notes that the IRS Commissioner who appeared before members of a Senate committee was subject to intense questioning as to how the figure concerning illegal drugs was reached, because it was well below that expected – indeed needed – by members of the committee in order to press home their arguments concerning the urgency of the drugs problem. The committee chose to accept the higher estimate provided by the Drug Enforcement Administration, an agency, it could be argued, with a vested interest in overestimating the scale of the drugs problem. While the IRS estimation appears to be based on more solid data than those of the President's Commission, the techniques used by the IRS are nonetheless open to challenge. However, this case is a timely reminder that criticisms of an academic or professional nature are not the only ones which matter. As was demonstrated here, political imperatives may be the most telling factor in the acceptance or not of research findings of this kind.

The proceeds of illegal transactions – as, indeed, all transactions – must have an outlet. They must be spent or invested. Modest amounts of money can be used in everyday transactions, or may be deposited in ordinary bank accounts, but amounts of larger proportion must be handled with greater care. The high returns from the trade in drugs, for example, need to be invested in business. The amounts are too large to spend. The process whereby illegitimate money, the proceeds of illegal activity, becomes legitimate, is known as 'laundering'. In the United States, banks are required by law to report domestic transactions of $10,000 or more, and foreign currency transactions of $5000 or more. While the law is regularly subverted in this area, many of those with the proceeds of illicit activities at their disposal prefer to 'launder' their cash through foreign banks or companies. The money is smuggled out of the country much as the drugs were smuggled in. The preferred depositories are 'tax haven' banks such as those of some of the Caribbean countries. Corporations are set up through which the money passes and its real history disguised. The money can then re-enter the United States or Europe without any suspicions being aroused. So commonplace have such transactions become in the public mind that they can be drawn upon by thriller writers, such as Elmore Leonard, in *Glitz*, as the central theme of a plot.

Attempts to measure the scale of this activity have suffered from the same difficulties as other estimations of clandestine activities. A study prepared by the Ford Foundation (US Congress, Senate Committee on Governmental Affairs, 1980) put the figure at $50 billion a year. Another figure, an upper limit of $43 billion, was mooted by the US Senate Committee on Governmental Affairs (1983). This Senate study reached its conclusion by taking one estimate of the size of the underground economy that included criminal as well as 'off the books' activity. It then assumed that the foreign commerce proportion of the underground economy would be equal to the proportion that foreign trade represented of the regular economy.

Those studying various formal employment-related aspects of the informal economy, such as pilfering, fiddling and other kinds of cheating at work, have come up with a variety of figures as to its value. One of the highest estimates for the UK was put at 1.8 per cent of the value of the visible economy (Outer Circle Policy Unit, n.d.). An American study extended the notion of theft to include time on the job! Thus an idle or lazy employee is actually 'stealing' from the employer. It was somehow estimated that the theft of time cost United States companies $125 billion in lost output in 1982 (quoted in Mattera, 1985:62). This is, perhaps, the most absurd – and extreme – attempt to estimate the volume of informal economic activity which we have come across. It does, however, provide a nice example of two themes which run, in differing degrees, through much of the literature we discuss in this chapter. First, there is the desire to express as much human activity as possible in economic, and specifically pecuniary or monetary, terms. This having been done, there is, second, the attempt to measure it 'on the ground'. They are each related to the other, to the crass materialism of much conventional economics and to the bureaucratic logic of control inherent in the modern state. These methodological issues – of valuation and measurement – are usefully discussed by Smith and Wied-Nebbeling in the context of the 'black economy' and the 'self-service economy' (1986:27–42). Before moving on to discuss attempts to quantify the size of the informal labour force, we will conclude with a couple more attempts to estimate the value of the hidden economy.

The wide variation in rates of taxation upon cigarettes between states of the United States was at one time significant enough to make the large-scale smuggling of cigarettes between states a very profitable activity. For example, in 1969 the purchase of cigarettes in North Carolina, which had no excise tax on tobacco, for resale in New York, could yield a profit of $66,000 for one lorry load of cigarettes. It was estimated that this practice was worth $100 to $170 million in 1975 (*Wall Street Journal*, 1976). The practice was curtailed by the narrowing of tax differentials between states. It is particularly in a case such as this that we see the distinction between legitimate activities made illegitimate because of the non-declaration of income for tax purposes and illegitimate activity, made illegal by the law of the land, beginning to blur.

Finally, attempts have also been made to estimate the income generated from the piracy of 'cultural products and brand name goods'. This extends from the makers of denim jeans who add the Levi-Strauss label to increase the consumer value of the product, to the illegal recording (bootlegging) of records, tapes and videos in contravention of copyright laws. One estimate has put the annual value of the pirate video business in London alone at £100 million (*The Times*, 1983), although this particular trade has since declined following technological innovations in the manufacturing process. Another increasingly profitable area of the bootleg industry is that to do with computer software. International differences with respect to either copyright law and/or the will or ability to police it adequately, can result in a situation, such as pertains in some Far Eastern countries, where bootlegging is a significant part of the highly visible – if not necessarily formal – economy.

Estimating the informal labour force

Two main approaches have been used in the attempt to calculate the size of the labour force working in the underground economy. One has been to compare two different methods used to compile official employment statistics. The other has been to examine various categories of statistics on the official labour force and look for unaccountable increases in the numbers in those categories from which the informal economy worker is most likely to come.

A popular method for determining the size of the unofficial labour force in the United States has been to compare the Census Bureau's Current Population Survey (CPS) estimate of the numbers of jobs and job-holders, with the Bureau of Labor Statistics survey of establishments of all sizes to determine the number of people on the official payroll. The CPS includes a monthly sampling of about 60,000 households in which questions are asked about the work status of their inhabitants. Figures are thus compiled from two very different sources. The comparison of the two sets of data is premised on the assumption that those working in the informal economy will declare themselves, or be declared, as job-holders in the household survey, but will not show up on the books of business enterprises. The discrepancy in numbers between the two is then taken as the size of the unofficial labour force, with changes between the two sets of figures being taken as an indicator of the rise or fall of the extent of underground economic activity. The assumptions underlying this approach are similar to those informing the comparisons between reported income and reported expenditure, as discussed earlier in this chapter.

Contradictory findings have been forthcoming using this method. Denison (1982) found that there had been no unusual changes between the two series of figures covering the years 1947 to 1979, and thus that there was no evidence of an expanding informal economy. However, O'Neil (US Congress, Joint Economic Committee, 1983) did identify a slight upward tendency in the figures for those in jobs as against jobs occupied according to business returns. This led him to put forward an estimate of 1.7 million people working in the underground economy full-time.

Mattera argues that the problem with this method is the need, in the first place, to establish a normal relationship between the two sets of data in order to establish that a change in the ratio between the two is a reflection of an increase in the underground economy. There is also the problem, already mentioned, of the acceptability of householders' responses. The assumption that those working in the informal economy will be declared as in a job is, for example, dubious. They might just as often be described as unemployed respondents, for whatever reason. Mattera points out that survey results of this kind can be skewed in a variety of ways.

Denison counters the charge that the validity of his conclusions is subject to speculation by relating the relationship between the two series of data to the size of the overall population. He found a consistent relationship between each of the series and the total number of people in the United States over 14 years old since 1947. Mattera, however, points out that

Denison does not acknowledge that the figures on the total size of the United States population are as contentious as those on the size of the labour force. For Mattera, estimates of the size of the informal economy based upon this source are as unreliable as those attempting to give it an accurate monetary value.

Turning now to the second method for establishing the size of the underground labour force, the search for unaccountable increases in those categories of workers in the official labour force statistics from which underground workers are likely to come, Italian economists have estimated that as many as 5 million people in that country work in the underground economy full-time (del Boca and Forte, 1982). A further 2 million, with jobs in the formal economy, are believed to supplement their incomes with undeclared second occupation earnings. Less attention has been paid to estimating the size of the underground labour force in the United States or United Kingdom using this method, because the attention of economists and government officials has typically been focused on trying to estimate the underground GNP. Mattera has, however, analysed the data from the two countries (1985:132–7).Central to this analysis are the following categories: self-employed worker, non-employed, unemployed and illegal immigrant. Mattera finds increases in each of these categories (with the exception of 'moonlighters' and illegal immigrants in the United Kingdom, for which categories there are no figures available) which indicate the size of the underground labour force. Warning that it is not realistic to expect that all the increases in these categories should be taken as an indicator of a rise in underground activity, he argues that only about half the increase should be so interpreted. This means that in the United Kingdom the size of the underground labour force would come to about 2.5 million (having taken account of the need to add in a few thousand for 'moonlighters' and illegal immigrants).

In all, Mattera favours a figure of 10 per cent for unofficial labour as a proportion of the official labour force. The figure is large enough to be significant but not, he feels, a sign that the unofficial labour force is taking over from the official one. These conclusions are subject to most of the provisos which have so far governed our interpretation of other ways of estimating the informal economy. They are only estimates at best. They are estimates which are subject to all kinds of methodological difficulties. Nevertheless, at various points there seems to be a correspondence with the findings from various sources. Whether this is significant or not is another matter. What is a common feature among most of these reports is that they agree that the level of informal economic activity, if not actually on the increase, is at least staying the same.

Regional variations in informal economic activity

The methodologies discussed so far, those relating to currency, income/expenditure discrepancies, profit from crime and labour force figures, have typically examined a particular variable in order to reach conclusions about the magnitude of underground economic activity. Next, we shall discuss an approach which began in this vein, seeking to establish the relationship between rates of taxation and participation in the underground economy, but was subsequently modified to take account of a wider range of variables which were felt to have a potential impact on underground economic activity. Frey and Weck (1981) ranked a number of the industrialized nations in terms of the tax burden placed upon their citizens. They expected to find a correlation between levels of taxation and the estimated size of the country's informal economies. They ranked the United Kingdom the tenth most heavily taxed nation, after Sweden, Norway, the Netherlands, Denmark, Belgium, Austria, Germany, Finland and France. Taking into account levels of taxation and legal regulation, the United Kingdom ranked fourth highest in terms of its putative informal economy after the Netherlands, Germany and France. The problem that Frey and Weck encountered was one of comparability: the estimated size of the informal economy varied greatly for countries largely according to the method of quantification which was used in each case. Taking taxation and regulation into account, Italy would appear to have a very small unofficial economy. However this contradicts conventional wisdom, which insists that Italy has a very large unofficial economy (see Weiss, 1987). It would appear that some account must be taken of cultural factors and/or the strength of the state, as revealed in the likelihood that people will pay their taxes. In Italy, despite the comparatively low levels of taxation, it seems to be the case that people are more willing – or more able – to evade paying taxes than, say, in Switzerland, where, despite comparatively high levels of taxation, the unofficial economy appears to be comparatively small.

As a result of this exercise, Frey and Weck concluded that a variety of factors had to be off-set against one another in order to arrive at any vaguely accurate estimation of the size of a nation's unofficial economy. In their own work they decided that they needed to balance, on the one hand, taxation levels, the effectiveness of legislation and regulation, individual attitudes towards paying taxes and their understanding of the system, with, on the other, the impact of the labour market and job vacancies, in order to reach any conclusions about *which* countries had *what* size 'shadow' economies. With commendable caution, they did not attempt to express these relative sizes in terms of monetary values. They estimated that the United Kingdom had a small informal economy, in contrast to the Netherlands, Belgium and Austria which were said to have very large unofficial economies, Italy and France which were said to have large unofficial economies and the United States, Finland, Japan and Switzerland which were said to have very small unofficial economies. The evidence for Canada, Sweden, Denmark, Norway, Iceland, Germany and Spain was, they decided, inconclusive.

The comparative approach of Frey and Weck has been adopted in order to try and take account of regional variations in informal economic activity in the United Kingdom (Button, 1984). Like Frey and Weck, Button makes no attempt to measure either the scale, or changes in the scale, of informal economic activity. Instead, he considers those factors which are likely to cause regional variations in its growth over a period of time. Button suggests a number of factors which are likely to influence changes in the volume of 'irregular' economic activity in any one region. Some of these factors were common to all the regions under study and so for the purposes of this comparative analysis were ignored. Those that remained include: an increased availability of resources to work in the irregular economy (as a result of unemployment, reduction of working hours, lower rates of pay in the formal economy), an increased burden attached to participation in the formal economy (related to different rates of taxation between regions and government controls over the nature and conditions of employment), an increased isolation from the formal economy (due to lack of contact with conventional employment markets as a result of prolonged unemployment), and an increased demand for the services offered by the hidden economy (the irregular economy is likely to grow more in areas where the growth of wages in the formal sector is retarded because the services it offers are cheaper as well as providing an additional source of income to supplement low wages). Button acknowledges that the direct measurement of these causal variables is not possible and so employs a number of operational indicators which, although not corresponding directly with the causal effects outlined, 'do provide data against which the basic, non-parametric methodology can be tested' (1984:387).

Data on seven variables were collected for the standard regions of England plus Scotland and Wales for the years 1977 and 1981. These variables were: unemployment rates, economic activity rates, working hours, household income, tax burden, government regulation and duration of unemployment. These variables were weighted according to a variety of schemes so as 'to test the robustness of the ordering of the regions with respect to the likely magnitude of changes between 1977–81 in their irregular economies' (Button, 1984:389). Regions were ranked separately according to each weighting scheme. In addition, the mean and median ranks for each region were computed, together with absolute deviation in mean rank. The results imply that greatest pressure for increases in the scale of the irregular economy between 1977 and 1981 was manifest in the North, Yorkshire and Humberside, the West Midlands and Wales. There seems to have been least pressure for an expansion in the informal sector in the North West, the East Midlands and the South West.

Button's purpose in this piece of research was as much to experiment with a 'fairly simple methodology' which might shed light on regional variations in the informal economy. The latter is merely the vehicle for his experiment. However he does provide us with a pioneering insight into possible reasons for intra-country variation as regards informal economic activity, the 'soft' nature of his analysis notwithstanding.

An even simpler methodology is employed by Smithies (1984) in his essentially descriptive account of the 'black economy' in England between 1914 and the late 1960s. Using local newspaper reports of court cases relating to black economic activity in six towns he attempts to document changes in its volume and character. These reports were drawn upon to estimate the number of cases coming before the court, whether their seriousness was changing, whether a market was created and whether the authorities ever lost control of the situation. Smithies concludes that throughout the period black economic activity remained small scale and, in terms of its financial rewards, out of all proportion to the amount of effort and ingenuity invested in it. A market was not created nor did the authorities ever lose control of the situation. In fact, at times the black economy could only function with the tacit approval of the authorities.

Smithies' account is unique in that it attempts to trace the development of the black economy in certain specific localities over an extended time span. But what of his research method? This is certainly a unique attempt to measure the informal economy. However, even setting aside the fact that he uses a narrow definition of black economic activity – equating it with illegal activity – there are shortcomings in his approach.

First, the six towns were chosen more for their diversity than their typicality (Smithies, 1984:5). Comparisons between localities and generalization from these to the whole of the United Kingdom are therefore difficult. At best his method could establish change over time in particular locations.

Second, the choice of newspaper reports of court cases as a reliable measure of black economic activity through time is questionable. Smithies himself notes that 'the figures of court convictions for the black economy crimes (obtained from local newspaper reports) are not a measure of all the black economic activity that took place' (1984:6). Many offences would not have come to light; some of those that did would not have been prosecuted. Smithies acknowledges that newspaper reports are usually of more serious black economy crimes. In order for reports of serious black economy-related crime to be useful as a yardstick by which to measure changes over time the policing of the black economy would have to have remained essentially the same, attitudes towards the prosecution of black economic activities would have to have remained constant and so would editorial policy towards the reporting of such activities. Smithies does not discuss these issues. In fact, he has little to say about his method at all. It would appear impossible to control for the affects of any such changes in practices and attitudes. In the light of the shortcomings of his method we feel that his conclusions, although interesting, should be treated with caution.

Returning to differences *between*, rather than *within*, countries, a recent study by Smith and Wied-Nebbeling (1986) has compared Britain and West Germany with respect to the dimensions of their 'shadow economies'. Looking at the 'black economy' (all illegal, informal economic activity) and the 'self-service economy' (everything from housework to voluntary organizations), they rely mainly upon a comparison of data derived from direct approaches, as discussed in the next chapter. One aspect of their work which is relevant here, however, is their use of income/expenditure differentials, particularly with respect to the self-employed, for purposes of national comparison (1986:69–73).

Two other things of interest for our discussion emerge from their analysis. First, in this as in other things, the non-comparability of official statistics and secondary data renders international comparison a hazardous business, at best. Second, as the above implies, the centrality of state regulation as *the* defining feature of informal economic activity is also problematic. The nature and boundaries of legal and administrative regulation vary from state to state. As a consequence, so does the nature of informal activity. A good example of this is what is called in Germany *Schwarzarbeit* (literally, 'black work'), i.e. carrying on unregistered business activity, the concealment of paid employment or working as a self-employed manual tradesman without the appropriate qualifications. Some of these are, in themselves, specifically illegal in Germany but not in Britain. As the authors point out, this raises two problems for their comparison:

Firstly, one empirical question, the extent to which business is carried on in contravention of the laws prohibiting *Schwarzarbeit* has no counterpart in the UK. The only relevant question in the UK is the extent to which economic activity in the UK is accompanied by tax evasion, and the investigation is most usefully organised according to the areas where scope for tax evasion arises.

The second consequence of the lack of a law prohibiting *Schwarzarbeit* in the UK is that customer accounts of the black economy in the UK might be expected to be more reliable than in Germany. The German law...puts both the supplier and the supplied...on the wrong side of the law;...failing to declare sales or income for tax in the UK usually involves only the supplier in any illegal action.

(Smith and Wied-Nebbeling, 1986:65-6)

Thus not only is informal economic activity differently defined and structured from country to country, but, as a consequence, national data may be correspondingly more or less reliable. Such obstacles to comparative analysis notwithstanding, they conclude with the suggestion (1986:88-9) that the shadow economy in each country is likely to be approximately equivalent in terms of volume and value.

Weiss (1987), writing about Italy, comes to broadly similar conclusions. She argues that the development of a significant clandestine economy depends upon the availability of certain structural resources – 'a dispersed economy, labour market segmentation, and a dense system of social networks' (1987:216) – themselves determined by historical processes largely influenced by the state. This suggests that 'the potential for the organization of clandestine production is not equally distributed throughout Western capitalism' (1987:231). The crucial determinants are not factors such as the incentives supplied by fiscal burdens or economic recession, the factors which are most often stressed in informal-economy measurement and which may be similar between countries, but rather social structural resources largely controlled by the state, which are inevitably different from country to country and which have generally been ignored in such research.

To summarize these various attempts at the comparison of informal economic activity within and between countries, a number of factors have been proposed as important to our understanding of regional differences in this respect. Labour-market conditions, the economic climate, culture and values, the organization and structure of legal and administrative frameworks and the power and nature of the state all seem to be influential. Inasmuch as comparative research of this kind represents a move away from crude (and speculative) quantification, towards an attempt to understand differences at the level of social practice and its interaction with the organization and institutions of the state in any given setting, this would seem to be a fruitful direction for further inquiry.

Plotting a decline in informal economic activity?

The work of Frey and Weck, Button, and Smith and Wied-Nebbeling marks a departure from the other methods and approaches discussed in more than one respect. In addition to focusing explicitly on a wide variety of possible factors which may stimulate informal economic activity, they are also concerned to highlight and understand variations between geographical areas rather than generic increases in underground economic activity as a whole. The research of Pahl in one area of the United Kingdom, the Isle of Sheppey, has led him to suggest that informal economic activity may actually be on the decrease in parts of the United Kingdom.

Pahl suggests five reasons why informal economic activity may be in decline (1984:93–8). First, while it is generally agreed that the self-employed generate the most undeclared legitimate income, he points to a decline in the numbers of self-employed during the 1970s: in the United Kingdom between 1975 and 1979 the population of self-employed workers declined from 1,875,000 to 1,795,000. The same trend is, he argues, apparent in the United States, where the number of self-employed professionals and businessmen – those who are probably in the best position to under-report income – declined from 20 per cent of the labour force in 1947 to less than 10 per cent of the labour force in the early 1980s. It should, perhaps, be pointed out here, however, that other writers have pointed to a more recent apparent increase in the number of self-employed people and drawn the reverse conclusion (Boissevain, 1984:26–38; Smith and Wied-Nebbeling, 1986:69–73).

Second, Pahl argues that the dramatic increase in unemployment and the decline of manufacturing industry has led to a decrease in 'opportunities for using the work place as a place for trade or source of information in the informal sector' (1984:94). Studies of cheating at work were carried out almost exclusively in the late 1960s and early 1970s; Pahl suggests that the Outer Circle Policy Unit report which assessed the value of the informal sector as a result of pilfering, fiddling and cheating at work at 1.8 per cent of the GDP, may well have documented the peak of such activity. Between September 1979 and September 1982, 2.2 million jobs were lost, most spectacularly in the manufacturing industries where 21 per cent of all jobs were lost during that period.

The third reason Pahl offers for the decline of informal economic activity is that while those who were unemployed during the 1970s had good opportunities for engaging in informal economic activity without being detected, there has been a change in attitudes during the 1980s, possibly due to an ideological shift in the country as a whole in reflection of government policies. Those claiming unemployment benefit may now run a greater risk of being exposed by neighbours if they engage in remunerative employment which is not declared. Pahl is aware of the caution with which such a hypothesis should be offered, but feels that it is a significant factor, taking into account the evidence from his own research during this period and historical evidence from a similar period in the 1930s.

Fourth, Pahl argues that Her Majesty's Inspectors of Taxes have become more efficient. Special offices set up to investigate the 'black economy' have apparently been very effective. Extra revenue increased from £6.4 million in 1977 to £20 million in 1980 as a result of an increase in the number of such special offices. By way of an implied counter to this argument, it might be the case, as Smith suggests (1986:197); following Miller's observation (1979) that individuals are more likely to comply with a taxation regime if they think other people are also compliant, that anecdotal accounts of 'working off the books', together with the publicity accorded to inflated estimates of the size of the hidden economy, may actually encourage informal economic activity.

Finally, the very area of the informal economy which is most often excluded from attempts to enumerate its size, self-provisioning within and between households, is the area which *is* undoubtedly expanding. Pahl devotes a significant amount of space to detailing this activity, in reflection of the importance with which he views it. This work is given more detailed consideration subsequently, in our discussion of direct methodologies for researching the informal economy (Chapter 6) and types of economic activity (Chapter 7).

We shall conclude this chapter with a brief appraisal of an indirect methodology which has been employed to investigate the growth of the household economy. Gershuny (1977, 1978) uses time-series data concerning a variety of expenditure categories to show that there was a trend away from expenditure on certain kinds of services in the United Kingdom and towards expenditure on certain kinds of goods. He developed this argument and claimed that people were spending more on manufactured goods in order to produce more services for themselves. Using national statistics, Gershuny argued, for example, that the private ownership of cars had coincided with a decline in the use of public transport. An increase in television set ownership had likewise coincided with a decline in public entertainment. He acknowledged that this trend away from public provision and towards self-provisioning was not apparent for every kind of service, as, for example, in the case of the proliferation of take-away food centres, which would suggest an increase rather than a decrease in public provision, but argued that, overall, such national statistics lent weight to the idea of an increase in self-provisioning in society.

Pahl and Wallace have pointed out that such calculations have their shortcomings (1985:191). As regards Gershuny's findings in relation to motor transport, there is a certain ambiguity as to how one should interpret public expenditure on motorways, for example. Should it be taken as an indicator of expenditure for public or for private transport? They also point out that while Gershuny could demonstrate an increase in the ownership of particular kinds of domestic capital equipment, such as power tools, he could not demonstrate the degree to which such equipment was actually used. However, Gershuny's work on time-budgets, based on Mass-Observation data for Britain in the 1930s and BBC Audience Research data at different times during the post-war era, was to allow him to present his argument with greater confidence. By time-budgets, we mean records kept by respondents, generally in the form of pre-structured diaries, of how they spend their time over a given period. In the United States, comparable data were collected in 1965 and 1975 by the Institute of Social Research at Michigan University.

The criticisms which have been levelled at the time-budgets/capital endowment approach can be applied generally to those using indirect methods to analyse the informal economy. Pahl, for example, argues that, 'these sources were not designed to deal with the complexities and subtleties of informal work' (1984:213). Gershuny acknowledges (1983:46) that such a time-series/capital endowment approach should ideally be used in conjunction with the 'consumer survey' approach of Ferman *et al.* (1978), with which we shall deal in Chapter 6. This notwithstanding, however, it is the difficulty, common to all the indirect methods examined here, in moving from aggregated macro-level analyses of informal economic activity to an examination of the more local, small-scale *minutiae* of informal economic activity at the micro-level, which limits the usefulness of such approaches. They cannot distinguish the growth or decline of informal economic activity in, at best, any more than a general way. Indirect methods concentrate on demand rather than supply (Thomas, 1988:171); they cannot tell us which sexes, in which households, at which stages of the life cycle, belonging to which social classes, in which areas, are most likely to engage in informal economic activity. It is to these kinds of questions – and to the supply side of the equation – that direct approaches address themselves. We shall discuss these methods in the next chapter.

Before moving on, however, it may be useful to emphasize what has been an implicit theme running through this chapter. Indirect methods are inadequate not because, or not *simply* because, of their inherent methodological weaknesses. This may indeed be true in some cases, but there is a more general, and a more important, problem. Conceptually speaking, they are founded upon a series of errors. Inasmuch as most of these methods are predicated, first, on the assumption that there is such a thing as a hidden (or informal, black, or whatever) economy, second, on the assumption that it is in principle measurable, and third, on the assumption that it is possible to isolate variables which serve to indicate, albeit indirectly, the size of that economy, these approaches are irretrievably built on sand. The indirect approach is thought to be necessary precisely because of the hidden nature of this sphere of activity. However, because it is conceptualized as 'hidden', these methods and findings are – by definition almost – unfalsifiable. As a result, the fact is often overlooked that these assumptions are, at very best, highly questionable. The third, in particular, has been shown, in a number of cases, to be especially problematic in the purely methodological sense. In the context of indirect research approaches to informal economic activity, however, they are each bound up with the others in a tangled web of confusion, wildly divergent or contradictory findings (Smith and Wied-Nebbeling, 1986:27–42), and largely wasted research effort. It is perhaps the most telling comment of all upon the political attractiveness of the myth of the hidden economy that, in the face of all of these shortcomings, these research endeavours have continued for as long as they have.

Chapter 6

Direct Research Approaches

As we have already outlined in the opening remarks of the previous chapter, direct methods attempt to ascertain sources and amounts of hidden income through the intensive investigation of small samples of individuals. As with those methods which may be described as indirect, there is a tendency in discussions of this topic to focus on those approaches which attempt to quantify in monetary terms the informal economy. We shall extend this categorization, however, to cover all those methods which have been used to investigate directly informal economic activity, whether or not they have sought to ascertain its economic magnitude. In addition to methods developed in relation to the tax-loss perspective, we shall deal with social surveys which rely on the questionnaire and the interview, the more or less structured techniques which are, perhaps, most suited to the study of informal economic activity from the point of view of household consumption and production, time-budget analysis, which may also be suited to the study of the household, and participant observation, which has most often been used, and is perhaps best suited, for the study of work-place related informal economic activity, such as fiddling. We shall also include a brief consideration of the ethical problems encountered in research using such methods.

Matters of revenue: estimating tax loss

Mattera reports (1985:52) that the Internal Revenue Service

(IRS) in the United States has estimated that $14 billion worth of income was undeclared by small-scale entrepreneurs in 1981. Since 1963 the IRS has operated a Taxpayer Compliance Measurement Program (TCMP), through which it rigorously scrutinizes the tax returns of a randomly selected sample of about 50,000 taxpayers. The tax returns of these people are matched against supplementary information reports submitted by businesses and individuals where large amounts of money are concerned. This is not done as a matter of course with all tax returns, due to the amount of work with which the IRS had to deal. At the time of the work of Gutmann and Feige, which we referred to in Chapter 5, the IRS relied on its TCMP data to estimate the scale of tax evasion. In a special study (US Internal Revenue Service, 1979; 1983), the IRS combined its TCMP data with estimates of the unreported income received by the five million people who are believed to make no tax declaration at all.

By using the TCMP and the data in its Exact Match File (relating to those persons not having made any income tax return at all) the IRS was able to estimate the value of unreported legal-source income. The amount was substantial, but estimates varied widely according to different categories of income and earner. Voluntary reporting percentages were compiled by the IRS by expressing the amount of declared income as a proportion of the additional amounts detected by its estimation techniques. There was variation in the percentages for voluntary reporting but it was clear that one category in particular, 'informal supplier income', was particularly under-reported. Voluntary reporting for this category constituted only 20.7 per cent, whereas it averaged about 90 per cent for the other various categories of income taken as a whole.

The IRS recognized that this particular source of income generation required investigation, and commissioned a study from researchers working at Michigan University (Smith, 1987). Over 2000 American households were surveyed on their spending patterns by the Michigan research team. This marked a departure from the normal IRS practice of concentrating on income. Householders were trained in detecting when suppliers were likely to be operating 'off the books', and the value of household purchases from informal vendors and suppliers was compiled. In total it was estimated that in 1981 $42 billion was spent by American houses on informal goods and services. The biggest single category was approximately $12 billion on home repairs. The researchers made adjustments for the assumed levels of the business expenses of the informal suppliers and also took account of income voluntarily reported, as well as that received by those not reporting any income at all for tax purposes, an amount already estimated. On the basis of this exercise, the IRS arrived at the estimation referred to above: $14 billion in taxable income was not being declared for tax purposes by small-scale entrepreneurs (Mattera, 1985:52).

This method has its fairly obvious shortcomings. As regards the TCMP, the national pattern is inferred from evidence provided by a random sample of 50,000. This in itself is not necessarily a failing; it is, of course, a standard technique in the social sciences. As such, it is subject to the qualifications to which all such random samples are subject. However, as Mattera points out, it is a method which is only really suited to particular kinds of informal economic activity: 'It is best able to track down income for which some documentation exists somewhere' (1985:52). The accuracy of measurement is, ultimately, dependent upon the allocation of sufficient resources by the IRS to inquire into tax returns. Finally, transactions which remain unreported by both the vendor and purchaser of goods and services will, of course, evade detection.

The study of small business activity by the IRS through the Michigan study went some way towards limiting the significance of these shortcomings by turning its attention from income to expenditure. However, it rested on the rather dubious evidence provided by householders who were trained to guess when the businessman with whom they were dealing was keeping the transaction out of his formal accounts. Despite these criticisms, Mattera argues that the direct measures for the study of tax evasion developed by the IRS are the most reliable macro-level research techniques which have, as yet, been employed in this area. He considers – albeit, perhaps, somewhat optimistically – that only an effective census of the informal realm will be able to provide any more accurate measurement of the size of the informal economy.

While the IRS does not compare its figures with the overall official GNP, its estimate of $250 billion in unreported income for 1981 approximates to something more than 8 per cent of the official GNP, although the GNP statistics already contain an adjustment for the amount of unreported income detected by the TCMP (Mattera, 1985:53). This adjustment amounted to $37 billion in 1981; $37 billion of the $250 billion would, therefore, already be counted in the GNP. Rather than the informal economy amounting to 8.5 per cent of stated GNP, as these figures suggest, it should, in fact, be recognized that the GNP itself is understated by about 7 per cent, the amount of unreported income not revealed by the TCMP. Bearing these adjustments in mind, the direct measurement techniques of the IRS come out with the same figure as Gutmann's indirect measurement techniques: the 'informal economy' amounts to about 10 per cent of GNP, a figure which is also in keeping with impressionistic estimates. Mattera accepts this as a reasonable working estimate, which accords in broad terms with other estimates regarding the size of the informal labour force, as already discussed in Chapter 5.

Gershuny (1983:43-4) urges caution in interpreting the findings of Ferman *et al.* from Detroit (1978), which were the result of an approach similar to that of Smith's IRS study. Based on a random sample of households in one city, they may not be applicable to other parts of the United States, let alone elsewhere. The findings refer to the provision of services rather than the value attached to those services by householders; consequently, these households may rely more heavily on the provision of services from the formal economy than is suggested by the data. These criticisms noted, we must also draw attention to a further major methodological problem with household surveys of informal economic activity, a problem highlighted and overcome (they believe) by Pahl and Wallace (1985). This is the recognition of the possibility of response bias in household surveys of clandestine activities, arising from the reluctance of informants to admit to sanctionable activity and thus incriminate themselves. While much of the activity referred to by the Michigan research team was not illegal, some of it was, and its revelation might – in the eyes of the respondents – have had potentially adverse consequences for those involved.

Getting at 'the truth': the question of respondent bias

Ray Pahl and Claire Wallace included in their survey of households on the Isle of Sheppey questions designed to elicit information on paid informal work. In response to the question 'Do you do any own-account work for extra money?', only 4 per cent of households revealed that any members of that household did engage in such activity. Another 1 per cent acknowledged that they did informal work for an employer or firm who paid them. The importance of such findings is unquestionable, if they can be taken to be reliable. Pahl and Wallace, realizing the caution with which such responses needed to be treated, carefully selected 30 out of their total of 739 respondent households for more detailed in-depth interviews. In certain cases, these households were interviewed more than once by a different researcher in turn. Their initial findings were confirmed by these follow-up interviews. Additional corroboration was provided by informal observation in the area, made possible by prolonged periods of residence there, and the resultant in-depth knowledge of particular households. Their use of a variety of techniques produced the same result. They argue that,

> attempts to elicit information about second informal jobs, work for cash and all other possible ways of explaining participation in the so-called black economy produced remarkably few cases.
>
> (Pahl and Wallace, 1985:210)

In addition to counselling caution in the extrapolation of social survey results concerned with informal economic activity – bearing in mind problems to do with the representativeness of the sample in question, as well as the precise meanings of the interview questions and respondents' reactions to them – we must also, however, recognize the possibility of respondent bias. Pahl and Wallace are confident that whatever respondent bias there may have been in their work, it did not result in the under-reporting of participation in informal economic activity. We do not intend to question their findings here. We merely wish to stress the care with which household surveys into informal economic activity should be conducted. Certain of the procedures which one might recommend, i.e. follow-up interviewing of a small sample of households and informal in-depth observation in the area, are evident in the work of Pahl and Wallace. For example, the importance of participant observation is illustrated by Wallace's discussion of the role of fantasy in young men's peer-group discussions of working while claiming benefit

(1986:106–7). Without good local knowledge, any researcher might easily be misled by such accounts.

Edgell and Hart (1988) acknowledge the problems associated with relying solely upon respondents' evaluations in measuring their involvement in informal and illicit economic activity. The use of such an approach might encourage either over-estimations of involvement due to the bravado of informants or under-estimations of involvement where respondents fear detection. Both dispositions are recognized as present in the sample in their study of firemen. On the one hand 'the fact that firemen were prepared to do such work and talk about it suggests that informal work was very much "taken for granted" in the service' (1988:31). They imply that the exaggeration of participation by respondents might result. On the other hand, Edgell and Hart point out that the Chief Officer had, only a short time before the interviews, formally discouraged informal economic activity, threatening dismissal to those caught. There are, therefore, factors which are at work in opposing directions in this context with respect to the discussion of informal economic activity.

However, although we are also told that the Chief Officer subsequently modified his position, Edgell and Hart (1988:24) feel that their (very high) figures of 90 per cent of firemen having done some paid work outside of formal employment at one time or other and 60 per cent being currently so involved is more likely to be an under-estimate rather than an over-estimate. On what basis they reach this conclusion we are not told. Presumably they see fear of detection as more significant than, for example, potential status enhancement, although no grounds for this assumption are apparent in their account.

There are methods which may be used to minimize respondent bias in the actual interview process. One set of techniques was developed for researching the 'black economy' in another part of the United Kingdom: Port Talbot, South Wales. In his consideration of the problems of bias and evasion, Lee (1985) proposed two main means for minimizing respondent jeopardy, i.e. the respondents' sense of threat from the questions, in the interview situation. First, it is possible to frame sensitive questions in such a way as to lessen the likelihood that the respondent will evade the question or give false information. The respondent is encouraged to reveal his participation in sanctionable behaviour because that behaviour is presented as common-place, something which 'everybody does'. A question on clandestine activity, for example, may be preceded by comments about its widespread occurrence and non-importance. The respondent is more likely to respond truthfully if such potentially delicate topics are broached in this manner.

The second approach involves what Lee describes as 'de-jeopardizing' techniques. Here, the interviewer asks a direct question, while at the same time reducing the respondent's reluctance to respond truthfully. At its most basic, this may take the form of respondents being allowed to fill in the interview schedule themselves. Adopting a more sophisticated approach, the researcher may adopt the 'randomized response' method or the 'nominative' technique. Lee's paper deals with the application of both of these techniques to the investigation of informal economic activity.

'Randomized response' involves the presentation of a sensitive statement to a respondent in conjunction with a non-sensitive statement. For example, in Lee's own work a statement on undeclared earnings was paired with a statement about month of birth. The choice of which statement will be the one to which a response should be made is decided by the respondent using some kind of randomizing device. In Lee's case the turning up of odd or even playing cards was used. Having chosen the statement, the respondent is asked to make a truthful response. The interviewer does not know which statement was chosen, and so cannot record potentially incriminating evidence about particular individuals. Providing that the statistical probability of the selection of the non-sensitive statement is known, an estimate of the proportion of those responding to the sensitive statement can be calculated.

Problems exist with this approach. It is not straightforward. First, the margin for respondent error is great if they are confused about what they are doing. Given the complexity of the operation, this is not unlikely. Second, no checks are available to the interviewer to monitor the possibility that respondents may be answering the non-sensitive question in every case. Finally, the apparent ingenuity of the methodology might actually increase feelings of jeopardy in respondents, who may feel they are being tricked somehow. Lee argues, however, that the propensity of the technique to produce larger sampling errors may be offset by a reduction in non-response bias. He cites evidence that research using the technique in other areas has concluded that it is of positive value, providing it is carefully piloted, probability levels are thoughtfully set and respondent understanding and trust are assured. If, however, understanding and trust exist between researcher and subject, it seems legitimate to question the need for such a circumlocutory approach in the first place.

The randomized response method has been used by Lee in Port Talbot and compared with direct questioning in obtaining data on what Pahl and Wallace (1985) call 'shadow wage labour'. He found that the proportion responding positively to a randomized response question about receiving money for work without declaring it to the Inland Revenue or the Department of Health and Social Security was greater than the proportion, in the same sample, responding positively to a similar question when put directly during the course of an interview, albeit with a 'permissive' preamble. However, the difference in these proportions did not prove to be statistically significant, and Lee concludes that the randomized response technique appears 'to have some, but only limited, utility in the study of the black economy' (1985:18).

The nominative technique is a relative newcomer to the range of methods available for overcoming the under-reporting of sanctionable or otherwise sensitive behaviour in the direct questioning situation. A 'shadow sample' of those having a particular attribute is ascertained by asking respondents about the activities of their relatives and friends. Weightings are employed to account for the appearance of the same individual on a number of occasions within the shadow sample. This technique, originally developed by Sirken to study the incidence of rare health events (Sirken *et al.*, 1975), has been successfully adapted to study illegal drug use (Fishburne, 1980).

Fishburne's work includes an evaluation of the methodology. The degree of jeopardy is minimized in that the respondent is not revealing autobiographical details and the anonymity of both the respondent and the nominated other(s) is maintained. Correspondingly, the under-reporting of clandestine activity should be reduced. A larger sample is made possible by the technique, as a single respondent may make reference to a number of households, thus allowing for the possibility of a relatively lower sampling error. A greater coverage of the population is possible, because the technique may extend to include those often neglected or missed by household surveys (for example, people in institutions). To these advantages, Lee adds the fact that interviewers do not hold potentially incriminating records on individuals.

There is an obvious affinity between the nominative technique and the long-established ethnographic practice of the intensive use of key informants. Thus quantitative and qualitative approaches may complement each other in this context. Fishburne also outlines a number of disadvantages with this method, however. The technique does not readily permit the study of non-public behaviour, such as sexual activity, for example, or the study of those who are socially isolated. Without reliable information about the respondents' relationship with the nominated others, a correct weighting to control for the repeated appearance of persons in the sample is difficult or impossible to calculate. Respondents may reject the role of informant, and there is no means for establishing whether the activities of others are being over- or under-reported, or, indeed, accurately or truthfully reported. The scope for deliberate misrepresentation on the part of interviewees is obvious.

Fishburne used the technique in a national survey on drug abuse. The incidence of heroin abuse obtained was greater than that revealed by other research which had relied upon direct reporting, suggesting that the method had reduced under-reporting. The non-response rate was very low, less than 0.5 per cent of those interviewees responding to the nominative series of questions. The method evidently worked for Fishburne. However, she warns against the automatic transfer of this technique to the study of other subjects. Certain conditions need to be satisfied, following detailed pre-testing. The behaviour under consideration must be of a kind likely to be known to other people, and should be sufficiently noticeable to be easily remembered. Prior to the research it should be determined which reference group is most knowledgeable about the behaviour concerned, and which reference group is most willing to report that behaviour.

Lee notes that, to date, no work has put these principles into practice. He has, however, assessed the potential contribution of the technique for estimating the incidence of 'shadow wage labour', arguing that it may be particularly useful in researching this kind of informal economic activity. We noted earlier, in Chapter 4, that social networks are particularly important in establishing access to the market for informal work. We also noted that, according to Pahl (1984), the formally employed were in a better position than the unemployed in this respect. Jenkins (1982), following Wadel (1973), has further suggested that those without employment may have to tread a narrow path between avoiding casual work, and thus being labelled 'workshy' by their acquaintances, and engaging in 'off the books' employment, and thus being accused of welfare scrounging. These two sets of observations testify to the likelihood of others having knowledge of this form of behaviour, thus meeting Fishburne's criterion of an activity likely to be known about and remembered by others.

Pahl has documented the existence of high levels of gossip about shadow wage labour, leading to research expectations of its being rife (1984). However, as we have discussed above, the actual recorded incidence of informal economic activity obtained through Pahl's household survey was, in fact, low. Such over-estimation on the basis of informants' statements, found also in Golding and Middleton's (1982) estimates of benefit fraud, based on the apparent knowledge about others offered by respondents when compared to official estimates, appears to be a major problem with this technique. Lee suggests that this kind of bias may be rendered less significant if the researcher is careful to avoid asking questions about the general frequency of such behaviour before dealing with the specific details of nominated others. This should reduce the tendency among respondents consciously to ensure that they match their general estimates – in all probability, no more reliable than anyone else's – with specific information.

As regards Fishburne's condition about the identification of suitable reference groups, she points out that respondents seemed more willing to give information about friends than about relatives. She was, as we have noted, dealing with heroin use. There is good reason to suspect a qualitatively different response when dealing with a subject like 'shadow wage labour'. As Lee points out, it may be more possible to document patterns of supply as well as of participation.

For Lee, the potential usefulness of randomized response and nominative methods lies in their ability to reduce individual respondent jeopardy. They are, however, unable to alleviate collective jeopardy which, he notes, is conspicuous by its absence in the methodological literature. Respondents may be reluctant to reveal information on clandestine activity in their area, because of the negative impact which such information may have for those living in the area as a whole. A similar point applies with respect to family or 'community'. The researcher is faced with an ethical question, particularly if research is carried out in or on an easily identifiable area or group. Those in the area, or members of the group, may become subject to increased surveillance by the agencies of social control, for example DHSS fraud squads introduced into certain local offices. The effects of elaborate research procedures to ensure anonymity could amount to naught in the long run if those associated with a particular area or group are stigmatized whether or not they possess the sanctionable attribute.

The researcher has little control over how research findings will be used. The social costs of the publication of research have to be weighed against the benefits. As regards research into 'shadow wage labour' or other forms of informal economic activity, research can potentially do much to counteract unsubstantiated public speculation in the media and elsewhere, particularly with respect to levels of benefit fraud or 'scrounging'. However, it is equally possible that the media, for example, may distort research findings to fit the mould of existing preconceptions about such topics. To provide a relatively mild example here, one of the present authors wrote a short piece for *New Society* on the situation of the young unemployed in Belfast (Jenkins, 1978). In the article it was argued that 'doing a double', working while claiming benefit, had, in fact, many beneficial social consequences, and should not be stigmatized as undesirable. This appeared on the magazine's front page as 'Richard Jenkins on young welfare scroungers'; hardly in the spirit of the piece! If a 'liberal' social science magazine is capable of such a distortion, what then of the daily tabloid press?

Documenting daily life: the time-budget approach

The use of time-budgets has already received brief attention at the end of the chapter on in-direct methods. There it was pointed out that data collected by various agencies such as Mass-

Observation or the BBC, which had no specific interest in informal productive activity, had been used to gauge the level of domestic production, in relation to other forms of production, through time. More recent research has used the time-budget survey – the detailed documentation, using a diary approach, of how people spend their time – to inquire specifically into 'the changing pattern of economic and non-economic activities outside of the formal economy' (Gershuny and Miles, 1985:34). Respondents are required to keep a record of their activities over a defined period of time.

Gershuny and Miles, and other members of the Technology and Social Change (TASC) group at Sussex University, used time-budget diaries in their research to test the Jahoda (1982) hypothesis concerning the relationship between unemployment and levels of psychological malaise. Time-budget data revealed that unemployed men generally increased their participation in domestic activity following job loss. This finding can, of course, be interpreted in a variety of ways. It may be suggested, for example, that participation in domestic production is a realistic alternative to participation in formal economic activity. It was only as a result of supplementary information in the form of attitudinal data obtained through interviews that such increased domestic activity was found to reflect shortages of domestic equipment and money, rather than a renegotiation of the domestic division of labour or the intrinsic satisfaction that might derive from domestic work. Unemployed men did not positively value their increased participation in the domestic domain. That participation was typically the outcome of necessity. It did not adequately substitute for the satisfaction to be gained from job work in the formal economy.

Time-budget analysis is perhaps one of the most suitable techniques for the study of non-formal economic activity precisely because such activity most often takes place within the privacy of the home. A good example of the approach's possibilities is the research of Trew and Kilpatrick into the lifestyles of unemployed men in Belfast, as already discussed in Chapter 4 (Kilpatrick and Trew, 1985; Trew and Kilpatrick, 1984). Drawing some of their inspiration from the work of Gershuny, and, more directly, Miles, they used a combination of time-budgets and interviews to document the lifestyles and day-to-day activities of their respondents. The authors used cluster analysis – and this is one of the most interesting and innovative aspects of their research in this context – to sort their sample into four lifestyles. Having done so, they were able to draw conclusions about the relationship between the informal domestic work done in the household by unemployed men and a number of other factors. Furthermore, the research was explicitly designed to allow for the comparison of its results with Ian Miles' Brighton data. This is one of the few rigorous comparative studies of informal activity which we possess.

The Belfast time-budget study does have its shortcomings from our point of view, however. In the first place, as Kilpatrick and Trew themselves acknowledge (1985:214), their sample excluded those men 'who engaged in full-time employment outside the formal economy'. Second, inasmuch as they were primarily concerned with the relationship between psychological morbidity and unemployment, they collected no systematic information about the relationship between self-provisioning/ domestic work and household capital/consumer goods endowment, for example. Third, and more telling in the context of a discussion of methods, there is little attempt to place their data in a diachronic context. It is impossible to gauge whether domestic work has increased or decreased with unemployment. These remarks notwithstanding, Trew and Kilpatrick's work remains one of the most interesting studies of informal work within the household in the British Isles. The time-budget approach, relying as it does on a formal and replicable method, was particularly important in permitting the comparison of material from Northern Ireland and England.

However, the time-budget approach's usefulness is limited by the fact that checks on the reliability of the data produced are not easily incorporated into the method. Time-budget analysis is clearly best suited for use in conjunction with some other methodology, particularly the interview or questionnaire. The work of Gershuny and Miles on the unemployed in Brighton, while testifying to the usefulness of time-budget diaries in revealing the extent of domestic work among unemployed men, also illustrates the scope for misinterpretation had such data not been linked to attitudinal data from interviews.

Ethnographic research approaches

Another major piece of research into informal economic activity in Belfast was undertaken by Howe, a social anthropologist (1984; 1985a; 1985b; 1987). He interviewed in considerable depth 20 unemployed and 20 employed men and their families from each of two housing estates, one in Protestant East Belfast, one in Catholic West Belfast. The interview data were supplemented by ethnographic material deriving from extensive participant observation over a period of two years, and data on the structure of local labour-market opportunities deriving largely from surveys in each area. On the basis of this wealth of evidence, Howe is able to demonstrate, first, that 'doing the double' (working while illegally claiming social security benefits) is more prevalent in West Belfast, and second, that this difference reflects different local opportunity structures and labour markets.

Howe's research suggests that the likelihood of overlooking important features of local informal economic activity – as is arguably the case with the work of Miles and Gershuny or Trew and Kilpatrick – will decrease if participant observation forms part of the research strategy. This is the approach which we shall discuss in the final section of this chapter.

The ethical repercussions considered earlier, in relation to the publication of research findings from social surveys, of necessity figure prominently in our discussion of the ethnographic approach and participant observation. This method has been found to be particularly appropriate to the study of work-place associated petty crime such as fiddling and, indeed, Ditton's research into this phenomenon, already mentioned elsewhere, will loom large in our discussion. Much has been written in a variety of contexts about participant observation as a research technique. Here we intend to deal rather narrowly with the topic, concentrating on a consideration of its suitability for the study of informal economic activity in the work-place, in the household and in the community. The work-place will be discussed first.

Mars has described how his interest in work-place associated crime arose. It was not as a consequence of reading about the phenomenon, nor as a result of abstract speculation about the existence of informal economic activity in the work-place; it arose out of first-hand experience as a worker himself, prior to embarking on an academic career (Mars 1982:17–20). This experience stood him in good stead when he eventually undertook social anthropological fieldwork among North American longshoremen (Mars, 1974; 1979), among whom fiddling of various kinds was common, if not endemic. The topic of Mars' dockside research was general; fiddling was simply one aspect of the culture of the longshoremen. His subsequent study of work-associated crime (Mars, 1982) is a combination of his personal work and research experiences and retrospective analysis from the perspective of a variety of academic disciplines. With respect to the practical and ethical complications which such an under-taking may raise, Ditton (1977) provides us with some insights.

Ditton's research context was provided by the company – a bakery – that had given him temporary vacation employment while he was still a student. He became interested in the culture of the work-place, although not specifically from the perspective of work-related crime. On completion of his undergraduate studies, and prior to having his postgraduate research proposal accepted, he returned to the bakery as a worker. He notes that he already knew most of the men as a result of previous periods of employment there and thus he had none of the 'usual problems of getting permission, getting into the field, getting accepted, or getting going' (1977:5). The heady days of (relatively) full em-ployment in the early 1970s are recalled as Ditton talks of having management plead with him to stay on to help out during the per-ennial summer labour shortage, instead of leaving formal employ-ment to work as a postgraduate student on his research design.

Ditton describes how he developed covert participant observa-tion skills right from the beginning of this period in the bakery, although he did not know at this time that he was to concentrate upon work-place related crime. An important research strategy was to retire to the toilet to write down important snippets of information, as to do so in full public view would have aroused curiosity (cf. Whyte, 1955:344). This would have been damaging to the project during the period he was researching covertly. Gradually his frequent visits to the toilet aroused curiosity, but his eventual admission that he was in fact engaged in research made note-taking in public easier. He never wrote while others were talking, however, and was generally uneasy about making notes in public – and this was still at a time before he had decided to look at 'irregular' activities. It was only towards the end of the field research that the likely focus of his research, 'fiddling', became clear to him.

Concerning the ethics of this research technique, Ditton says that he was 'partially open' about his general role (1977:9), conducting interviews in a more formal way in addition to his participant observation. He justifies the subsequent publication of his findings in a number of ways. He protected the identity of the bakery and those he studied while working there by omitting names and changing facts which were not important to his study. It would not have been possible to disclose his full intentions during the research stage, since he was not clear about them until the latter period of his fieldwork; more generally Ditton suggests that *all* participant observation is, in some respect, ethically problematic (cf. Barnes, 1980:77-8). Covert participant observation is, of course, particularly problematic ethically (Bulmer, 1982).

In fact, *all* observation challenges the usual rules which govern interaction between human beings. Ditton's major technique was the 'fake question': the asking of a general question on some matter, to which the researcher can pretend to be noting an answer while in fact recording some other piece of information which has arisen concerning the topic really interesting the researcher, an interest unknown to others: 'Without reliance on some subterfuge the practices of subterfuge will not be opened to analysis' (Ditton, 1977:10). In a different context, Barrett has described an analogous approach as one of 'deceptive candour' (1984:9). Ditton cites Daniel's (1963) work on salesmen as a perfect example of ethical research. Daniel interviewed workers in a bakery, who disclosed that the salesmen were on the fiddle in a major way. He then interviewed the salesmen, who denied that they engaged in any fiddling. The groups' different levels of commodity consumption as regards personal transport (the fact that workers had bicycles and salesmen, cars) were explained by Daniel in terms of salesmen possibly having part-time jobs and the two groups possibly having different expenditure preferences. These were, Ditton suggests, the only ethically 'proper' conclusions possible. However, the issue here is not really one of ethics – or not solely ethics. It is not clear to us, for example, that an ethically attuned research strategy precludes a critical stance with respect to the veracity of one's informants. To be ethical one does not have to be naive.

There is, nevertheless, undoubtedly an ethical problem to be taken into account when contemplating this kind of research – whether covert or open – into informal economic activity – whether covert or open. While, in one sense, all observation breaks the implicit rules structuring social interaction, participant observation does not necessarily have to be covert. There are degrees of openness. In Whyte's (1955) classic study of an American slum, 'Cornerville', part of which focused on racketeering, the collusion of an 'insider' or key informant was invaluable to the research process. Access to street life would have been impossible without such a locally esteemed guide. The researcher became a member of a street gang and as such was able to observe at first hand activity from which he would otherwise have been barred. While his key informant, 'Doc', knew of his intentions, other gang members were not as fully informed. Community members were, by and large, simply told that he was 'writing a book' about Cornerville. Whyte also encountered the problem of how to record information on what were often illegal activities. Any opportunity to be in private was taken but much of the time he had to rely on memory. While Whyte's research could hardly be described as altogether open, nor was it covert. He did cultivate the complete confidence of one of those he was studying, for example, although the degree to which 'Doc' knew Whyte's full intentions may also be questioned. Part of the difficulty here stems from the fact that Whyte, as also Ditton, was not sure of the focus of his research until well into the fieldwork. It is, in fact, probable that Whyte, inasmuch as many of these things only become clear after the fact, *could* not have known fully what his *eventual* intentions were likely to be. The uncertain focus of much ethnographic research in this respect encourages a 'write it all down regardless' approach, which can create problems for researcher and researched alike (Jenkins, 1984a).

The examples of research cited so far are characterized by an interest in informal economic activity which arose incidentally out of research which had as general focus the culture or social life of an area or group. Participant observation was the major research technique. The suggested usefulness of participant observation in a research project designed specifically to deal with informal economic activity must, however, be qualified by an awareness of its limitations. As a technique it is ideally suited to the work-place, where the long-term presence of the researcher, either disguised or open, may allow the creation of a 'group member' identity to a greater or lesser degree. The technique is less suited to other contexts of informal economic activity, such as the household, for example. In small-scale residential communities, such as a village, it is sometimes possible, through long-term residence, to observe, or at least get to know about, informal economic activity within particular – although probably not all – households. The 'community study' tradition is well established in sociology and has its definite uses. Such an approach may also be possible in certain urban areas where interaction between residents, or members of a particular 'community', is sufficiently intense.

Participant observation, the traditional ethnographic approach, has definite limitations, however, with respect to the nature and the amount of social interaction to which it permits access in large-scale urbanized societies and communities. It is clear that the researchers' long-term knowledge of their area of research has materially aided four recent studies of informal economic activity in the United Kingdom, those undertaken by Pahl and Wallace in the Isle of Sheppey, Harris *et al.* in Port Talbot, Turner *et al.* in central Scotland, and Howe in Belfast. However, in all of these cases participant observation was used in conjunction with extensive data obtained through interviewing. In-depth knowledge of particular households merely strengthened the researchers' belief in the validity of their statistical or interview data, as in the case of Pahl and Wallace's findings – already discussed – about the level of paid, undeclared work for others in the Sheppey study. It would, we believe, prove difficult, if not impossible, for participant observation to be the main means for researching self-provisioning or 'moonlighting', for example. It is more suited to researching the more contextually delimited topic of 'fiddling' on the job.

One final point about the appropriateness of participant observation as an approach needs to be made, with respect to the study of crime, that informal economic activity which is inherently illegal. This may be the category of informal economic activity for which this methodological approach is most appropriate. Participant observation may, however, draw the researcher into participation in non-lawful activity, at the risk of coming into conflict with law enforcement agencies. Certainly, both of the present authors, in separate pieces of research among young people (Jenkins, 1983, 1984a; Reynolds *et al.*, 1983), have confronted this problem. The extent to which researchers allow themselves to be associated with such potentially sanctionable behaviour is a matter of personal judgement, about which no categorical statements can or should be made. Such judgements are dependent upon the perceived seriousness of the activity, a moral dilemma facing any person with respect to extra-legal activity with which he or she may come into contact. Polsky, for example, has warned that in the study of criminal behaviour it is essential for the participant observer to make his or her research role known, in order to avoid getting 'sucked into "participant" observation of the sort you would rather not undertake' (1967:122). The alternative – covert research – involves exposure to risks which may have even more drastic consequences for the cause of the research, let alone anything else.

While on the subject of research ethics there are also related issues of disclosure and public pronouncement to be considered. If we are correct in the arguments offered in this book – that the hidden economy model is theoretically naive and empirically unsubstantiated – then those social scientists who have promoted it and advanced it in the counsels and discourse of politicians bear a heavy responsibility. Social science research and theory do not, of course, necessarily (or even usually, perhaps) exercise an influence in these circles. When, however, academics provide politicians with ammunition or legitimation in the pursuit of their policy goals they are, quite naturally, welcome on board. Equally naturally, academics in such a situation may be glad of the encouragement, particularly at a time of financial retrenchment and institutional restructuring. As a consequence, over-enthusiasm – albeit well-intentioned – may result in poor judgement. The disjuncture between Pahl's early enthusiasm for the notion that the 'informal economy' was a haven for the unemployed (1980), and his subsequent – and admirably honest – disavowal of that position following the full analysis of his research data (1984; 1988), is only the best-known example. It is, however, salutary and should stand as a reminder of the perils of precipitate publication.

To conclude this discussion of research methods, both direct and indirect methods for the study of informal economic activity have their shortcomings. The particular strength of direct approaches is that they are actually designed to generate data on informal economic activity, rather than make sense of already collected material. As such, direct methods can be tailored to meet the need of a particular research problem. They allow for the much greater qualification of findings within a sample population. The time-budget survey appears to be the technique most suited for studying certain aspects of informal economic activity; participant observation, however, is more suited to looking at other aspects. What is clear is that such methods should not be used in isolation, they should be supplemented by the use of an interview schedule or questionnaire.

A recent contribution to the debate on the informal economy (Gershuny, 1985) has stressed the need for research into the development of household work strategies using sociologically grounded methods which can take account of the extra-economic factors which contribute to economic structures. This work is already well under way in Great Britain (Pahl, 1984). Direct approaches may, nonetheless, be as vulnerable to criticism as the indirect approaches discussed in Chapter 5, inasmuch as they are, in some cases, founded upon what we have called 'the myth of the hidden economy'. Informal economic activities can be documented, they can be compared and, in many cases, they can be readily quantified. That does not make them a 'hidden economy', however. Nor can this supposed 'economy' *as such* be either documented or measured.

It further follows from this that there is no one method or approach which is the 'best' for research into the 'hidden economy'. Although a direct approach may be more defensible than an indirect, this is not to say that some indirect methods do not have their uses (particularly, as we argued in Chapter 5, in the drawing of regional and national comparisons). Of the direct methods, each with its own advantages and disadvantages, some are more suited to the examination of one kind of informal economic activity, some to another. It is often the case that direct methods are best used in combination with each other, in order to document most comprehensively the range of informal economic activities in any specific social context. In the next chapter we shall look at different categories of informal economic activity in more detail.

Chapter 7

VARIETIES OF INFORMAL
ECONOMIC ACTIVITY

At the end of Chapter 4, in Figure 1, we introduced a simple framework within which to discuss various forms of informal economic activity. We have argued that this model is potentially more useful than the proliferation of models of separate or multiple economies criticized in Chapters 3 and 4. In Figure 2, following, we locate 14 types of economic activity in relation to degrees of formality or informality, on the one hand, and notions of work and employment, on the other. In this chapter we shall consider these forms of economic activity, all of which – even formal waged employment – partake to some degree in informality, under nine headings, as follows:

1. self-employment
2. the household
3. the community
4. homework and outworking
5. between work and employment
6. informality on the job
7. formal waged employment
8. corruption
9. crime

These categories are differentiated thus for purely heuristic reasons. The difficulties – both theoretical and in research practice – involved in drawing clear boundaries around different types of economic activity have been made sufficiently clear in preceding chapters. We are not, of course, able to overcome them in one fell swoop, nor would we necessarily wish to, given the complexities of the situation. Our argument, however, is that the location of various activities on a map of formality/ informality and work/employment, as in Figure 2, allows for considerable flexibility in the categorization of any particular activity. Such a scheme permits the relationships between economic activities of various kinds to be specified and represented diagrammatically. This, in turn, may facilitate the aggregation of sometimes disparate economic practices under one heading without over-structuring or reifying the fluidity, and frequently improvisatory nature, of everyday social practices. Thus we are enabled to connect a particular practice with one set of activities under a given set of circumstances, while relating it to other types of activity in a different context.

In the discussion which follows, we shall look at each of the nine headings above in turn. Drawing on a selection of the available literature we shall attempt to put some meat and sinew on the bare bones of the skeleton outlined in Figure 2. In so doing, however, it is not our intention to achieve a comprehensive coverage. Instead we hope to proceed by way of simple and apt illustration towards a more rounded picture of the varieties of informal economic activity. It will be noted that the descriptive categories in Figure 2 do not correspond exactly to the nine categories of economic activity listed above. Figure 2 is, in fact, a slightly more detailed expansion upon those basic categories, as will become clear in the discussion which follows.

Working for yourself: small businesses and self-employment

Self-employment illustrates clearly the difficulties involved in classifying economic activity. Drawing a distinction between self-employment and other forms of formal economic activity is possible. Employment, as we have defined it, involves wage labour and the control and direction of one's productive practices by another. Self-employment is characterized by the nominal absence of such features. The differences were made clear in Chapter 2. However, the boundaries begin to blur once we start talking about self-employment in the context of informality. On the one hand, we immediately encroach upon categories such as household economic activity when considering unpaid family labour and the small business; on the other, forms of self-

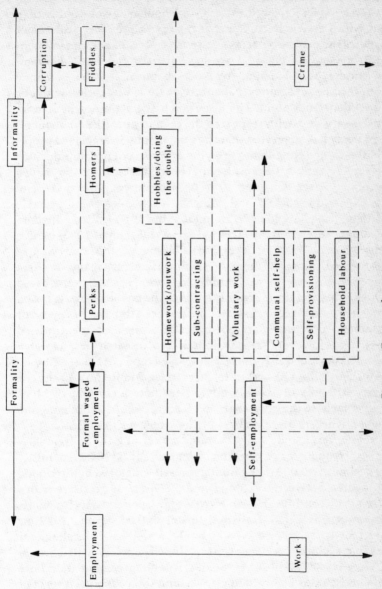

Figure 2 Forms of economic activity

employment begin to take on the mantle of 'hobbles' – to use an expression local to South Wales – or labour-only-sub-contracting, in which a strictly commercial relationship between customer and client may also partake of some aspects of the employment relationship. In Figure 2 we have tried to represent diagrammatically the blurring of such boundaries, the semantic imprecision and contextual nature of these categories, with our directional indicators. The use of such a device is nowhere more necessary than with respect to the category of self-employment.

Handy has suggested that the number of self-employed people in the United Kingdom is growing by 5 per cent per annum. Such economic activity belongs to what he has described as the 'mauve economy' (see Chapter 4). The workforce is 'betwixt and between the formal and informal economies, a respectable fringe' (Handy, 1984:47). He quotes the 1982 United Kingdom Labour Force Survey (*Employment Gazette*, June 1983) which discovered 75,000 workers in addition to those previously estimated, most of them in small businesses, many of them operating from home. Handy lists 26 possible home-based businesses and these are only some of the possibilities. As tax on the self-employed is collected in arrears after the first year of trading, such people are not necessarily engaged in extra-legal activity. However, we have alluded to research in Chapter 5 which concluded that the self-employed tend not to keep Pay-as-You-Earn (PAYE) accounts, nor to question too closely the circumstances of those whom they themselves employ. It is reasonable to suppose that this feature will be more common when workers are members of the employer's family.

However, Handy's observations concerning the self-employment trend have not gone unchallenged. Pahl (1984:94) points to a decline of 80,000 in the number of self-employed in the United Kingdom between 1975 and mid-1979. He suggests that this trend will continue. However, as we have pointed out elsewhere, inasmuch as Pahl's statistics do not extend beyond 1979 his argument is, at best, weak. Smith and Wied-Nebbeling, for example, point to a 20 per cent rise in self-employment in Britain between 1979 and 1983 (1986:69). This disagreement underlines the difficulties involved in establishing the volume of a form of economic activity for which even the most accurate statistics are somewhat unreliable and which fluctuates over time in response to other factors. Self-employment can be said, in retrospect, to

possess one or other characteristic – formality or informality –
according to whether taxes are eventually paid on the preceding
year's business or not. However, if we take into account the
conditions under which the self-employed, and those whom they
employ, often work, and the general low degree of state
regulation of their activities, it appears that much self-
employment may come under the rubric of informal economic
activity, whether or not income is declared or taxes eventually
paid.

Much attention has been paid to the motivation of those who
become self-employed. Many of those starting an independent
business do so to 'escape from the constraints of authority, the
wage-profit relationship and other features of being an
employee' (Scase and Goffee, 1980:35). Pahl suggests that a
combination of self-employment with wage labour is possible,
being particularly prevalent in the building trade for example
(1984:123). Scase and Goffee, in their search for an entrepreneurial 'type', conclude that a particular attitude towards the
employment of the labour of others is a major characteristic of
the small business owner, having priority over other factors such
as views on profit maximization or attitudes towards taxation
(1980:161–2). Small business owners may often be reluctant to
expand their operations in directions that would require them to
employ people in a wage relationship, because they feel
constrained by employment legislation, although doubts about
what the market will bear or their own managerial ability may
also figure prominently in their reasoning. Expansion tends to
take place in directions which do not require them to employ
wage labour. Scase and Goffee suggest that where workers are
employed by small businesses, more, rather than less, government legislation may be needed, since workers in small
businesses are likely to have to endure low pay, poor working
conditions and are usually non-unionized. The basic motivation
of many of those who set up small businesses conflicts with the
interests of those whom they employ.

There is, however, another characteristic common to many
small businesses. This is the tendency to depend upon some
unpaid family labour. Such a strategem may be particularly
common in rural societies and in agriculture, in the form of the
family farm (see, for example, Errington, 1986; Long, 1984), and
among ethnic minorities in the United Kingdom and elsewhere

(see, for example, Ward and Jenkins, 1984). Scase and Goffee (1980:90ff) point, however, to the indispensability of unpaid family labour for the survival of most small businesses, regardless of ethnicity or field of operation.

The dependence of small-scale farming on family labour has been well documented by many community studies in different parts of the British Isles. Whatever the deficiencies of community studies in conceptual or methodological terms (Bell and Newby, 1971), they provide much valuable data on social, economic and political life at the local level in both rural and urban areas. Arensberg and Kimball's pioneering studies in Ireland (Arensberg, 1939; Arensberg and Kimball, 1940) reported the propensity for small farmers to use as fellow workers, 'family and the co-operative group of friends' (Frankenberg, 1966:27). Williams reports that 75 per cent of the male labour on farms in 'Gosforth' was provided by farmers and their kin (not necessarily all of whom were household members), while for female labour the figure was as high as 95 per cent: 'The predominance of the ideal of a farmstead which can be run without paid assistance is such that it appears to over-ride purely economic considerations' (Williams, 1956:38). Such a significance was attached to the self-sufficiency of the kin group that low productivity often resulted. The pattern is repeated in other community studies, differing only in the degree to which unpaid family labour is mixed with wage labour. For example, in Wales in 1931 farmers and their relatives made up 80 per cent of all male persons engaged in agricultural work while for females the figure was 90 per cent (Frankenberg, 1966:48). Even those who were hired as wage labourers tended to be the kin of their employer. Later studies of Welsh rural life reveal a diminished, but nonetheless significant, use of family labour (Frankenberg, 1957; Rees, 1951).

More recent work on small-scale farming in the United Kingdom has shown that reliance on unpaid family labour is still important for the rural economy. Interestingly enough, evidence from an area of East Anglia where 'agribusiness' is well established suggests that the larger the unit the more likely it is that family labour – in particular sons – will be involved in running the farm (Newby *et al.*, 1978:67–9). Many of the smaller farms cannot economically absorb a son's labour. A young man in this position must seek employment elsewhere until he comes into his inheritance. On most small farms, it is the wife who provides the major additional family labour input.

Despite technological innovation and a tendency for large-scale farms to replace small units, the family farm continues to survive, however, particularly in the dairy production sector. Bouquet, in her study of family farms in south-west England (1984), explores the differences between the labour of men and the labour of women. She notes that women have become largely excluded from traditional farming productive activities, both agricultural and dairy, during the last hundred years. Farming has come to be regarded increasingly as men's work; women's domestic labour in the farming unit now far outweighs any labour they put into farming activities as such. However this development does not mean that females are excluded from productive activity altogether. Bouquet describes female domestic labour as coming in two forms in south-west England. On the one hand, unpaid labour for the 'family', which involves servicing the domestic domain; on the other, paid domestic labour in relation to visitors who are taken into the household as paying guests during the tourist season. Women's increasing marginality to traditional productive activity on the farm has been matched in some localities by an increase in their contribution to production through accommodating tourists, thus providing a crucial additional source of cash income to the household. Newby *et al.* have also described the important 'business' role of women, providing a whole spectrum of office and administrative services on farms (1978:68). In addition, women engage in voluntary work which serves to bridge the gaps in provision created by the lack of commercial interest in rural areas and the absence of adequate welfare provision. Through their activities, women provide indispensable resources to a traditional 'small business'.

Unpaid family labour, then, remains an important dimension of both large- and small-scale farming. The reliance upon unpaid family labour among ethnic minorities in business in the United Kingdom and elsewhere has also been well documented. Aldrich *et al.* (1984:196-7), in their study of Asian and white shopkeepers in three English cities, found significant differences in the degree to which the two groups used family members and relatives, particularly extended family members and often unpaid. They found that Asians were much more likely to use such labour and also discovered that a higher percentage of Asian than white

respondents were themselves the sons of self-employed businessmen. There was apparently a greater tradition of self-
employment among Asian shopkeepers.

The contribution of cultural factors to the success of ethnic
minority businesses has often been alluded to. Boissevain, for
example, notes that ethnic minority entrepreneurs in the
catering trade,

> succeed not just because European demand for exotic food is
> growing. The hard work, long hours and family labour with
> which they have developed ethnic catering throughout
> Northern Europe are important resources when they compete
> directly with their hosts (1984:35).

One of the present authors, in outlining directions for further
research into ethnic minorities in business, has proposed that the
relationship between business life and the domestic domain
should be explored in more depth than hitherto. This suggestion
applies as much to businesses belonging to the majority (white)
population as to those of the ethnic minorities:

> Clearly if we are to understand, for example, the role of the
> Asian extended family, or family labour in ethnic minority
> business generally, we must be able to bring comparative data
> for white-owned businesses to bear on the discussion.
>
> (Jenkins, 1984b:235)

More generally, Scase and Goffee make the important point
that there is a range of costs, both social and personal, for the self-
employed person and his/her family, whatever his/her ethnic
origin or geographical location (1980:107–8). This feature of self-
employment is likely to be particularly pronounced during the
initial stage of setting up a business, or in times of reduced
demand. For the self-employed person, work and family are
intimately connected: hierarchy within one sphere may equal
control within the other. The maintenance of family relationships may be essential for continued economic success.

In summary, self-employed people and small businesses are of
particular interest from the point of view adopted in this
discussion. First, for the self-employed the relationship and
distinction between work and employment is in many circumstances unclear. This is most obviously the case with respect to
family labour. Second, many small enterprises straddle, with

greater or lesser degrees of comfort, the grey area – if the reader will forgive the near lapse into colour-coding – between the formal and informal. In both respects, this category of economic activity may be viewed as, in some senses, paradigmatic of the central issues with which we are concerned in this book. This is all the more the case if one accepts the likelihood that, in the currently high-unemployment economies of the capitalist social democracies, the proportion of economic activity accounted for by small businesses and self-employment is, even if it does not increase further, unlikely to diminish.

Domestic work: the household and family relations

For Scase and Goffee, small-business households or families are in a situation which other households and families are not, namely that no strict demarcation between work and family life is possible. We would suggest, in considering our next category of economic activity, that to do with the household, that they overstate this tendency. A blurring of work and family life may be a feature of many households whose members are not self-employed.

We have already noted the introduction of the notion of 'household work strategies' into the sociological literature (Gershuny, 1983:47; Pahl, 1984:131–9). Even outside the entrepreneurial family/household, household labour, it is argued, is frequently organized not merely to meet basic domestic needs, but also to provide members of the household with final services which might otherwise be obtained for cash from those outside the household. What is more, argue Gershuny and Pahl, such self-provisioning is on the increase. To domestic labour (what has been called reproductive activity) must be added self-provisioning (production for one's own, or one's household's, consumption). The idea of a household work strategy encompasses these two types of activity but is not equivalent to our category 'household economic activity'. Household work strategies involve the provision of services to meet the household's needs from extra- as well as intra-household resources.

For Pahl, household work strategies need to be understood in relation to the domestic cycle and the sources of labour that are available within any household at any given time. It is, therefore, impossible to generalize about the form which household work strategies take. There is nothing intrinsic about any particular activity which consigns it to the household category. Pahl illustrates this point by taking activities such as ironing a garment (1984:123–6) or repairing a roof (1984:156–8) and looking at the range of social relationships within which such activities may be undertaken. What is important is who carries out the work, and for whom. For example, the ironing of a garment by a woman may be regarded as household economic activity if the woman is ironing her own garment, in order to wear it for her next day's wage labour, for example (in which case, Pahl describes it as 'individual reproduction'), or if she is ironing the garment for another member of the household, so that he/she can wear it to his/her place of employment (in which case it is termed 'social reproduction' by Pahl). As regards the repair of the house's roof it is only household economic activity when a member of the household undertakes the task. Where the roof is fixed by friends, neighbours or relatives, that is where the consumer is not the producer but the cash relationship is not the sole and central feature of the transaction, then informal communal sources of labour are involved. This corresponds to what we term community economic activity, as discussed below.

Before leaving this topic, there are three important dimensions of household economic activity which remain to be discussed: first, the gendered nature of domestic economic activity, second, its relationship to the labour market, and third, the fact that it may be both formal and governed by an employment relationship. We will look at each of these in turn.

With respect to the first issue, both commonsensical observations and a number of influential research studies (Gavron, 1966; Myrdal and Klein, 1968; Oakley, 1974a, 1974b) insist that economic activity within the household – *house*work – is largely *women's* work. Bound up with a gendered division of emotional labour which stereotypes women as more 'caring' than men (Finch and Groves, 1983), this aspect of, to continue with Pahl's categorization, social reproduction, is a major, or even *the* major, strand in the role of 'wife' and 'mother': cooking, cleaning, not only producing children but bringing them up, being responsible for clothing, attending to the management of much of the mundane routine of domestic life and providing emotional succour and support. There is considerable recent research to suggest that this extends to the management of the unemployment of children and male partners (Hutson and Jenkins, 1987; McKee and Bell, 1985; Morris, 1985; Popay, 1985).

It is not, of course, that men do *not* engage in household informal economic activity; as the discusssion above has implied, they do. What we are saying is that they do less, and only particular kinds of things. Just as there is 'women's work' so there is 'men's work': fixing the car, vegetable growing, house maintenance, etc. The gendered division of domestic labour resonates with, and is informed by, wider social models of gender roles; the distinction may also be characterized as between continuous work (female) and discontinuous work (male). It is not, of course, the case that the 'traditional' division of domestic labour is adhered to equally strongly within all households. Changes in women's consciousness and socially acceptable gender roles have had some influence, albeit small. It might also be thought that a combination of higher female economic participation rates and male unemployment will lead to a renegotiation of the domestic division of labour. Recent research into this topic, however, indicates that, in fact, male unemployment leads to little or no change in this respect (Clark, 1987; Hartley, 1987; Morris, 1985).

The influence of unemployment upon the domestic division of labour brings us to the relationship between household economic activity and the 'external' labour market. For men, this relationship is generally straightforward: the demands of the labour market are pre-eminent, work within the household coming second, and sometimes a very poor second.

For women, however, the relationship between the two is more complex. In the first place, despite an increase in female economic participation rates in the United Kingdom and elsewhere since the Second World War, it remains the case that women, whatever their own view of the situation might be, continue to bear the major responsibility for the care of children and men (Martin and Roberts, 1984:96–115, 169–84). This has consequences for the kind of employment they undertake (Land, 1981). For example, much female employment (formal and informal) is in occupational categories which are homologous to their 'service' role within the family: nurse, cook, cleaner, primary school teacher, the 'caring' occupations and professions, prostitute, etc. (Dex, 1985:79–111; Hakim, 1979). This has important consequences for the skill and status which are seen to attach to such jobs. Similarly, inasmuch as primary domestic responsibilities usually fall to (particularly married) women, and are typically perceived as having first call on their time, many female employees either 'choose' or are channelled into part-time work or work whose hours suit their household situations (Martin and Roberts, 1984:34–42; Yeandle, 1984: 107–32). Among the variations in this 'flexibility' is homeworking, which we shall discuss further below.

The nature of women's labour-market careers is also a result of the assumption or imposition of household responsibilities, particularly with respect to child care. Social values and institutional arrangements being what they are, having children means, for most women, a break in their employment, which, in turn, means lost promotion or training prospects, among other consequences (Freeman, 1982; Mackie and Pattullo, 1977:96–112; Martin and Roberts, 1984:116–37). Women's labour-market discontinuity may also be a result of male occupational mobility; it is typically the case, for the reasons which we have outlined immediately above, that women move with men's geographical employment mobility and not vice versa.

The relationship between female household economic activity and the labour market, as reflected in occupation, hours of work and employment continuity, has one further important dimension. As a result of these factors, among others, women's wages are on average significantly lower than men's (Dex, 1985: 112–42; Joshi, 1984; Martin and Roberts, 1984:43–59). This aspect of women's labour-market disadvantage is encapsulated – once again, despite what many women think themselves and the reality that households typically depend on women's wages as part of an overall domestic economic strategy (Coyle, 1984; Pollert, 1981; Yeandle, 1984) – in the notion that women work for 'pin-money'. In the situation which pertains in an increasing number of households, headed either by a woman single parent or with the husband unemployed, 'pin-money' may be the main family income source. The interaction between labour-market participation and household labour responsibilities is a major constraint, what is more, upon the pursuit of equality of opportunity for women (Chiplin and Sloane, 1982; Curran, 1985).

Our final word with respect to women's household economic activity and the labour market concerns the 'domestic labour debate'. What is at issue here is the role of the unpaid labour of women in underwriting part of the costs of the social reproduction of the capitalist labour force, hence maintaining wages at an artificially low level. In other words, what would employers have to pay (male) employees if those employees themselves had to pay for the (women's) household work upon which they depend for their sustenance and the production of future generations of workers? The issues raised by this question have important implications for Marxist theory and the theorization of the relationship between gender and stratification (Harris, 1983:179–200; Molyneux, 1979; Rushton, 1979). Suffice it to say here, however, that the domestic labour debate is another indication of the necessarily intimate relationship between informal household economic activity and the 'external' labour market. The consideration of this topic is given a further twist by Finch's research into those, typically professional (male) jobs in which the unpaid work of the wife is a recognized part of the package which the employer is buying (Finch, 1983).

Finally, it should be remembered that the labour market may, on occasions, intrude very directly into the domain of household economic activity. Whether formally or informally, people – and it is usually women – may be employed as domestic servants, nurses, nannies, companions, or whatever. One might also stretch the point to include such situations as local authority funded fostering and respite care. Whatever the actual situation, however, the general point holds good: household economic activity may, in particular contexts, be organized within a formal employment relationship.

To reiterate the major concerns of this section, our discussion of household informal economic activity highlights three important themes. First, gender roles and relationships are as influential – if not more so – in structuring informal economic activity as they are with respect to formal economic activity. Second, the relationship between the household and the labour market, whether formal or informal, is one of close interplay and reciprocal interpenetration. Finally, inasmuch as this is the case, the organization of household economic activity must be seen as a major factor contributing to the social production of patterned gender inequalities and, more broadly, the stratification system.

Social networks and the community

The overlap between our categories continues as we come to community-based informal economic activity. We have mentioned this category already in the context of both self-employment and household economic activity. We include both communal self-help and voluntary work under this heading and in so doing approximate to Gershuny's (1983:34) idea of communal production. Voluntary work, in particular, involves a range of activities which span formality and informality, work and employment. We will examine in more detail Pahl's illustration of informal communal labour in order to illustrate what we mean by communal self-help. We shall then go on to look at voluntary work proper, as described in the writings of Pahl (1984), Handy (1984) and Bouquet (1984).

In discussing household economic activity we were dealing with intra-household exchange. Community economic activity encompasses 'the question of inter-household exchanges and community-level patterns of co-operation' (Long, 1984:17). These exchanges and patterns, are, of course, the routine subject matter of much rural sociology and ethnography. They have also long been recognized as a feature of established urban working-class communities, not only in the form of the co-operation between a mother and her daughters, who may be living in separate households (for example Aschenbrenner, 1975; Leonard 1980:223–55; Young and Willmott, 1957), but also between the household and relatives on both mother's and father's side and between neighbours (Bott, 1971; Bulmer, 1986; Stack, 1974). While geographical proximity enhances the effectiveness of such relationships (Rosser and Harris, 1965:14) physical distance does not mean that such relationships are ineffectual. We use community, therefore, in a broad sense, not simply as an indication of geographical proximity. Community may also be defined in terms of criteria of group membership which do not require constant geographical proximity; ethnicity is an obvious example of such a membership criterion. Telecommunications and modern transport enable regular contact to be maintained over what might previously have been regarded as insurmountable distances. The functioning social networks of a British ethnic minority community may, for example, span the length and breadth of the United Kingdom (Bhachu, 1985; Tambs-Lyche, 1980).

For Pahl, the essence of communal sources of labour is that social relations are based on informal ties between producer and consumer. As already discussed, he uses the example of roof repairs being carried out by friends, neighbours or relatives. The relationship between consumer and producer is not analogous to that between employer and employee. It can only be regarded as such by ignoring factors other than the passage of money between the two parties. The relationship is *qualitatively* different from that of employment: 'The norms of reciprocity and a complexity of social relationships surround the transaction' (Pahl, 1984:137). Payment may be in kind, it may be deferred for many years – in which case the profit motive may be absent – it may also be in cash. In this sense it is powerfully influenced by norms which are very different from the formal and informal rules governing transactions in the formal economic mode of exchange. This does not, however, mean that such transactions belong to a separate economy. Nor does it mean that the relationship is uncoloured by economic norms and motives.

Were, however, the roof to be fixed by a firm of builders, then the source of labour would be completely different: 'The consumer interacts with a workman hired by the employer whom the customer pays' (Pahl, 1984:138). From the point of view of the particular form of informal economic activity under discussion, the communal, it is irrelevant whether the employer declares this income for tax purposes, employs his wife as unpaid labour in the running of the business, or whether the workers hired by the builder are also claiming unemployment benefit. The activity is employment based upon the wage-labour relationship. The fact that the builder may not be declaring income for tax purposes, may employ his wife as unpaid labour in the running of the business or the worker hired by the builder may also be claiming unemployment benefit is a matter for consideration under the category of self-employment elsewhere. This is a good example of our attempts to keep the categories of economic activity analytically distinct, and a pertinent illustration of the difficulties attendant upon doing so. These difficulties are thrown into sharp relief by considering, for example, the case of roof repairs carried out by a neighbour who is a professional roofer, but who charges the householder a reduced 'cash in hand' fee.

Pahl's observations on voluntary work are interesting. He

wishes to keep 'voluntary work', which may be done anony-
mously and which is not based upon the 'constraints of
interpersonal interaction or related to any reciprocal recompense'
(1984:124), distinct from activity which he describes as 'social
solidarity work'. Returning to his example of a woman ironing a
garment, were she to be carrying out this activity for a colleague
in a local dramatic production, or for a sick neighbour, and was
doing so by choice, without coercion of any kind, it would be
described by him as 'social solidarity work'. For the moment, we
shall use the term 'voluntary work' in Pahl's sense, consigning his
'social solidarity work' to our category of communal self-help.

Handy (1984:19) suggests that voluntary work, or what he
describes as 'gift work', may occupy as many as 18 million United
Kingdom citizens for at least an hour a week (Humble, 1982),
equivalent to the labour of 500,000 full-time workers. Nor is it
confined to women, the middle classes or the elderly, as popular
stereotypes might suggest: 'Gift work is a part of everyone's life'
(Handy, 1984:56). The extent of voluntary work and its
distribution among the population is not, however, an issue here.
Rather we are concerned in the first instance with its relation to
formality and employment, and, in particular, its meaning for
those who undertake it.

Bouquet makes reference to the 'good cause' in her study of
south-west England: 'Good causes are distinguished by the
events they generate, usually through a voluntary association
directed towards some "community" goal' (1984:152). They may
benefit people living locally or may be designed to benefit some
wider population. In Bouquet's study this kind of activity is the
province of women. Female competence is, to a great degree,
measured according to performance within the fund-raising
field. There is, of course, scope for the manipulation by
individuals of this type of activity. Status can be enhanced within
the community. At the very centre of the 'good cause' one finds,
as Bouquet observes, the very opposite orientation to 'community spirit', the pursuit of individual advancement. While
community economic activity is often not governed by economics
in the narrow sense of the term, a certain social economics
appears to be operative in determining decision-making and
behaviour. The costs and benefits, in a social sense, which are a
consequence of certain courses of community action are
considered by those engaging in such activity.

Voluntary work is not merely a matter of communally defined costs and benefits, however. The 'voluntary sector' is an important aspect of welfare provision and social service delivery in the capitalist social democracies of the West. Historically speaking, the growth of the modern welfare state can be seen to be rooted in the unco-ordinated activities of a wide range of voluntary organizations which had – or have – their origins in nineteenth-century liberal ideologies of self-help and charity for the deserving poor. These voluntary organizations have not, however, necessarily atrophied or declined in size and importance with the development of formal state welfare provision. Nor is all non-state welfare provision organized via the voluntary sector. Four points, in particular, require emphasis.

In the first place, on surveying the spectrum of ends or objectives to which organizations in the voluntary sector address themselves, the most striking impression is of diversity: everything from famine relief in the 'third world', to the prevention of cruelty to animals, to nature conservancy, to adoption, fostering and child welfare. In terms of the scale of their operations, they vary from the strictly local, to the national, to the international and multinational. In terms of the means by which their ends are approached, once again there is considerable diversity: lobbying, direct intervention, indirect intervention through the provision of funding to other agencies, all these have their place. It may, therefore, be sensible to recognize that the 'voluntary sector' (much like the 'informal sector', in fact) is *at best* a heuristically useful category with which to lump together a diverse heterogeneity of non-state practices and organizations concerned with 'doing good'. At worst, the notion reifies and over-structures the reality of the situation. To make matters more complicated, it is also clear that it is impossible to say where voluntary work ends and pressure-group politics begins, if at all. Nor, as we shall discuss in Chapter 8, are leisure and voluntary work easy to disentangle in many contexts.

Second, the sources through which voluntary work and voluntary agencies are funded are threefold. The state may provide subsidies, as may international organizations such as the United Nations; transfers from the wealthy (and sometimes the not-so-wealthy) through bequests, tax-deductible donations and foundations are often important; the general public may also provide resources via appeals, flag-days, second-hand shops, jumble sales, etc. Any combination of these three basic sources is possible. All of these possibilities require the existence of formal organizational structures and, in particular, accounting and financial procedures. They also require, in all cases, licensing and monitoring by the state. As a consequence, while many of the individuals who work for voluntary organizations do so informally and without remuneration, they are nonetheless integral parts of a formal, bureaucratic set of practices.

Third, the state itself intervenes in a more complex way in the area of voluntary work, particularly at the level of the 'community', and even more particularly at the level of the *working-class* community. Through the medium of such relatively new 'caring' professions as community work and youth work, local voluntary activities and organizations – everything from mothers and toddlers groups, to action groups organized around specific local issues, to groups of young people doing painting and decorating for old-age pensioners – are 'developed' and 'facilitated'. Through a process of 'need' identification, to 'intervention', to 'organization', and, perhaps, eventually to 'evaluation', community workers liaise with existing community groups and encourage the foundation of new ones (Henderson and Thomas, 1981; Twelvetrees, 1982). Typically funded, either directly or indirectly, by the state, and working within the constraints implied by such funding, youth and community workers are, increasingly, themselves the product of licensed, higher education training courses. Despite the important influence of a professional ideology committed to the enablement and political mobilization of working-class communities, community work remains part of an apparatus concerned with the containment of protest and the maintenance of public order, even if its relationship to that wider whole is complex and often contradictory.

Finally, much non-state welfare provision is completely informal and non-organized (which is not the same thing as *dis*organized). This is the domain of kinship and neighbourhood relations: family, friends and neighbours (Bulmer, 1986; Stack, 1974; Willmott, 1987; Young and Willmott, 1957). The importance of such informal social networks for the transfer and exchange of goods and services has been an enduring theme throughout our discussion so far. It is, therefore, interesting to note, in several countries, a coming together of social-work goals of enablement, de-institutionalization and self-help with the quest for acceptable cuts in ever-expanding social welfare budgets in the shape of 'informal care' policies (Bulmer, 1987; Walton, 1986, Willmott, 1986). This is a more complex issue than we can do justice to here. Suffice it to say that one important dimension of the issue, from the perspective of our discussion, is the attempt to integrate more closely formal welfare provision with informal social support networks. Once again, the distinction between the formal and the informal may be extremely difficult to establish in practice.

Employment on the margins: homeworking and outworking

The cash nexus is the fundamental element in social relations in our next category of economic activity: homeworking and outworking. Hakim, in her preface to Cragg and Dawson's (1981) research report on homeworking, suggested that there were in Britain between 200,000 and 400,000 homeworkers or outworkers, 'in the sense that they work in or from their homes for an employer who supplies the work to be done and (in the case of manufactured goods) is responsible for marketing and selling the results'. These figures are, of course, only estimates and must be treated with caution. What is clear, however, is that outworking is not restricted to the manufacturing sector; it is increasingly also a feature of service-sector industries (Lipsig-Mumme, 1973). Elsewhere, Hakim suggests that the number of blue-collar and white-collar outworkers is roughly equal (1980:1110). Huws (1984:14) argues that working at or from home, or from a neighbourhood work centre, is increasingly viable in financial terms because of the declining costs of telecommunications (1984:14). Handy sees a shift from 'trains to (computer) terminals' in bringing workers to their work, or rather, their work to the workers (1984:72-5).

A distinction can, however, be made between the manufacturing sector and the service sector concerning the degree to which *out*working is actually *home*working. Homeworking in the manufacturing sector in Britain amounts to well under 10 per cent of all outworking in that sector (Hakim, 1984:10). The majority of homeworkers are in white-collar or service occupations, where 'freelancing' is a more common description of their role.

Homeworking, and outworking in its white-collar form, under the label freelancing, tends to merge with the category of self-employment. Blue-collar outworking, however, tends to have many features in common with the labour-only-sub-contracting which we shall discuss in detail below. There is a strong subjective dimension in this labelling process, especially in respect to how people describe themselves to census enumerators. A white-collar worker appears more likely to describe him or herself as freelancing than a blue-collar worker, who might well describe him or herself as self-employed. Hakim (1985:68) notes the general tendency of outworkers to describe themselves as self-employed, despite the fact that they work for the same single employer, often for extensive periods.

Cragg and Dawson provide some interesting information on the subjective dimension of homeworking in their report *Qualitative Research Among Homeworkers* (1981). The decision to work was dominated by financial considerations for the majority of their respondents, who were women with husbands in full-time employment. A third of the sample regarded their income from homework as essential for the maintenance of their living standards. 'Fulfilment' was also an important factor, however. Homework apparently provided these women with a sense of usefulness and enhanced self-esteem, while relieving the rigours of being a child-bound housewife. However, a preference for working outside the home was commonly expressed, along with the hope that return to 'inwork' would someday be possible. In nearly all of these cases dependent children were the factor preventing this. There was an almost universal belief among respondents that mothers should be ever-present to rear children before and out of school.

The attractiveness of homework for Cragg and Dawson's respondents was increased because homework was regarded as a scarce resource. This perception helped to encourage their tolerance of poor pay and the monotonous nature of the work. The characterization of homework as low-paid and exploitative is firmly supported by other evidence (Brown, 1974; Crine, 1979; Hakim, 1987; Hakim and Dennis, 1982; Martin and Wallace,1984: 214–16; Rubery and Wilkinson, 1981). Poor wages and terms of employment are bound up with the informality of employment contracts and recruitment procedures (Leighton, 1983). In many cases (40 per cent) Cragg and Dawson's respondents had obtained the work through the introduction of a friend. A large proportion (34 per cent) had replied to press or shop advertisements while a number (14 per cent) had been invited to continue working as part-time homeworkers by former full-time employers. The importance of informal social networks for obtaining homework is confirmed by these findings, with at least 54 per cent of the subjects in this study relying on personal contacts to obtain work.

The relation of these workers to state regulation may be explored by looking at the way in which they were paid and their attitude to taxation. Between one-third and one-half of the sample were paid by cheque. The others were paid in cash. A substantial minority, about one-third, appeared to be given no pay slip or record of payment at all. The majority of respondents knew they were below the tax threshold. Only 8 per cent deliberately avoided paying tax and a further 10 to 12 per cent suspected they should pay tax but made no move to declare income preferring to leave the initiative to the authorities. Most respondents did not fully understand the tax system: 'Many of the respondents did not regard themselves as really *having jobs*' (Cragg and Dawson, 1981:21). Here is the notion of 'real work' again, as discussed in Chapter 2. Four per cent of the sample were claiming social security benefit while earning amounts in excess of the permissible amount without declaring that income, justifying their actions in terms of economic necessity. They were 'perturbed' by the possibility of their situation becoming known to the DHSS. Other respondents described homeworking as providing an income to supplement the social security benefit of unemployed husbands.

If the study by Cragg and Dawson may be taken as representative of the situation throughout the United Kingdom, homeworking appears to be an activity largely undertaken by housewives. The criterion for recruitment of respondents was that they

> should work at or from their homes, for gain and for an employer. Excluded from the sample were self-employed professionals, freelancers and tradespeople; and those who, by the nature of their work, necessarily combine business with living premises – for example, publicans, farmers or shopkeepers.
>
> (Cragg and Dawson, 1981:1)

The original target of 10 per cent males in the sample proved impossible to reach. Only one man (2 per cent of the sample) was interviewed.

On our map of economic activity (Figure 2), homeworking and outworking are centrally positioned. As economic activities they have the potential for movement in all directions, to more or less formality, to the world of work or the world of employment. Our main qualification to this observation is that homeworking is largely a female activity, because of the child-rearing role of women in the conventional family context. The gendered character of homeworking – rather than anything intrinsic to its nature or organization – must, we suggest, be regarded as the major determinant of its meagre economic rewards and peripherality with respect to the formal :abour market.

Homework as *women's* work is perhaps the most important theme of research in this broad area. However, a subsidiary theme – which we have already alluded to above in our references to the work of Handy and Huws – is the notion that, as part of a burgeoning 'information society' or a 'post-industrial society', homeworking offers a release from the dreary monotony of office or factory work, an opportunity for a degree of self-direction and autonomy. In this sense, homework may be conceptualized as lying somewhere between employment and self-employment.

We have already summarized a fair amount of evidence which suggests that this benign interpretation of homeworking is unrealistic. Allen and Wolkowitz, reporting their research into homeworking in West Yorkshire, provide one of the strongest rebuttals of the 'optimistic' view:

> Popular images of working at home – flexible working hours, more time to spend with one's children, a reduction of work pressure, a less stressful day – have nothing to do with the experience of homeworking. The women experience the two sets of constraints simultaneously on a day-to-day basis. Homeworking is very far from being a boon to women, for instead of liberating them from or reducing the burden of the 'double day', it intensifies the pressure of both waged work and unpaid domestic labour.
>
> (Allen and Wolkowitz, 1986:46)

They also document the necessary support which homeworkers

receive from spouses, family friends and neighbours, without which homework would often be impossible (see also, Allen and Wolkowitz, 1987). The point is, of course, that, as a specifically gendered form of informal or quasi-informal economic activity, located, by virtue of its very nature, within a gendered division of domestic labour, it is unlikely that homeworking could be anything other than poorly-paid and massively exploitative. Within the context of capitalist relations of production, the informality of homeworking, far from offering increased freedom or enhanced self-direction, is likely to be a particularly effective control stratagem. It is this central insight which is missed by authors such as Handy.

The final point to be made about homeworking is, to reiterate a more general theme which has been running through our discussion so far in this chapter, the degree to which our category of 'homework' overlaps with our other categories of self-employment, the household and communal economic activity. This is most critically the case with respect to the household, and it is in this coming together of domestic labour and wage labour that the key to the exploitation of women as homeworkers is to be found.

Between work and employment

Sub-contracting, although occupying a similarly central position to homework in our classificatory framework is more a male-dominated economic activity. It may, in fact, in important legal or contractual respects relating to the absence of a conventional wage relationship between the paymaster and the paid, be almost exactly analogous to homeworking. The difference is that one is within the household (female), the other is outside it (male). We shall deal with sub-contracting at the same time as 'hobbling', the South Wales term for the undertaking of undeclared economic activity (Morris, 1984:5), and its Northern Irish equivalent, 'doing a double', which means engaging in financially re-munerative work while drawing welfare benefits and being registered as available for employment (Jenkins, 1978). We conceptualize this constellation of activities as lying between work and employment.

Goldthorpe has argued that there is an increasing tendency for large-scale enterprises to transfer a part of their production, under sub-contract, to smaller concerns (1985:142). By sub-contracting, organizations are able to guard against the ill-effects of fluctuations in demand for their product because a permanent workforce does not have to be paid during slack periods. They are also able to avoid to some extent the rigidities of the labour market, including the bargaining power of the trade unions. Once again, informality in this context is, in large part, an important mode of control for employers.

This observation has been fleshed out by the work of Chris Harris and his collaborators in South Wales. In their research into the effects of large-scale redundancies from the British Steel Corporation (BSC) plant in Port Talbot, a variety of relationships between formal and informal economic practices was established (Harris *et al.*, 1987). As a part of the redundancy agreement, BSC undertook to encourage the employment of ex-steelworkers by those local contractors to whom they allocated the work previously carried out by BSC employees. The creation of redundants was to be paralleled by an increase in the demand for labour (redundant steelworkers) among local employers. The terms of employment in these new jobs, however, were much changed by comparison with BSC. Ex-steelworkers were employed to do fixed-term (and short-term) jobs. The type of contractor which was encouraged was one who employed 'irregular', 'lump' labour, paying non-union rates and not bound by national agreements (Fevre, 1983; Morris, 1983).

Morris (1984) illustrates the relationship between 'a hobble' and the acquisition of fixed-term work in this area of South Wales. What began as 'a hobble'–an informal job, 'off the cards'–for one of her respondents ended up as a 13-month-long 'legitimate' job. The man had initially obtained the work, with a contractor at British Petroleum (BP), through a friend's introduction and it was to last a couple of weeks only. However the need for his labour continued and the work relationship was formalized. The activity was transformed from 'a hobble' into formal employment because of the length of time that the work lasted.

A similar point has also been made, although in a longer time-scale, in connection with 'the double' in Northern Ireland. Howe, whose research we have already discussed in Chapter 6, argues that:

Perceived opportunities in the black economy (here I mean

only that part of the black economy in which unemployed people 'do the double') are inextricably linked to those in the labour market for legitimate jobs, and this is especially so in West Belfast.

(Howe, 1985b:10).

Howe's evidence suggests that in East Belfast, dominated by large manufacturing firms and public administration, there is little scope for 'doing the double'. Furthermore, inasmuch as the local economy has perhaps suffered less than other parts of Belfast, the unemployed may still look forward to a future of employment as a realistic possibility. In West Belfast, by comparison, in a labour market – such as it is – 'fragmented with large numbers of small companies, many self-employed trades-men and numerous small retail outlets' (Howe, 1985b:16), 'doing a double' is a much more likely proposition. In addition, the local economy in West Belfast is in such bad shape that informal economic activity of this kind, most frequently in the construc-tion industry, is viewed as a more likely option than employment.

It should, perhaps, be emphasized here that ethnic residential segregation is well established in Belfast and the possibility of sectarian violence is a real one. Mobility within the Belfast labour market is, therefore, extremely restricted (Cormack *et al.*, 1980). There is an important sense in which the unemployed residents in Howe's 'Mallon Park' housing estate are 'trapped' in West Belfast. The scope for their movement into other areas of the city in search of employment, whether formal or informal, is strictly limited.

These everyday realities have, Howe argues, an influence upon local cultural orientations. In West Belfast, 'doing a double' is seen as part of the way of life; it is accepted, even approved of. This is less the case in East Belfast. However, Howe is quite clear that these local differences should not, for example, be viewed as differences between Protestants and Catholics with respect to their orientations to work. They are, rather, the product of different social situations. The research of one of the present authors on a Protestant housing estate on the northern fringes of Belfast, where 'doing the double' appears to have been more prevalent than in 'Eastlough', Howe's housing estate in East Belfast, bears this out (Jenkins, 1983).

One difference between 'Eastlough' and 'Mallon Park' which may be related to sectarian divisions in Northern Ireland, however, is discussed in Howe's work. DHSS Fraud Investigation Officers may be less free to operate in 'Mallon Park' because of the local security situation. Similarly, local people may be less prone to providing the DHSS with information on neighbours whom they view as 'scroungers'.

Looking at the informal jobs outside the construction industry which were held by Howe's subjects, the majority were short-term and insubstantial. The same holds true for many of the construction jobs. The income from this informal economic activity was not an *alternative* to social security benefits, rather it was a *supplement* to state benefits. Here the importance of poverty must be stressed. There is, therefore, no sense in which there could be said – for these unemployed people – to be an 'alternative economy' in West Belfast. Nor, it is clear from Howe's research, have the unemployed – despite the local social acceptability of 'doing a double' – lost the 'will to work'. Such a view is also supported by other evidence from Northern Ireland (Jenkins, 1983:44-7, 68-79; Morrissey *et al.*, 1984:48-9; Tipping, 1982). The great majority of the unemployed continue to yearn, albeit perhaps hopelessly, for a stable, 'steady' job. In the absence of such a job, eking a living on benefit, the occasional 'double' may be all there is.

Whether work is regarded as 'the double' or 'a hobble' may depend, in part, upon the length of time that work lasts. One significant result to emerge from the South Wales study was the finding that while a man might continue to claim unemployment or supplementary benefit for a few days or weeks of 'hobbling', it was rare for him to continue claiming where he had accepted full-time employment over a longer period of time. In Northern Ireland, however, where the writ of the law may run less consistently and with less authority, a 'double' may be more long-term. It is, however, unlikely to be more secure.

Sub-contracting, 'hobbling' and 'doing the double' are not synonymous. It is on the basis of some of those features that they have in common, in particular the fixed or limited nature of the work, that we include them in our 'between work and employment' category. It is the nature or duration of the relationship between worker and contractor, or the fixed specification in advance of the job to be done, which are the criteria for internal differentiation within this category. The major criterion differentiating such arrangements from the other categories of economic activity discussed in this chapter is the insecurity of the relationship between worker and boss, and the consequent vulnerability of the former.

It is worth re-emphasizing that economic activity which is between work and employment should not be regarded as the sole preserve of the unemployed. In fact, certain forms of employment positively lend themselves to employees undertaking economic activity of this kind. Edgell and Hart (1988) confirm the impressions of earlier studies (for example Thomas, 1969) that firemen in Britain engage in informal economic activity on a large scale. The structure of the working week – 'both day-manning and shift workers had four full days and nights in every eight days off duty' (Edgell and Hart, 1988:26) – enables firemen to devote substantial amounts of continuous energy to such 'fiddle jobs', as Edgell and Hart call them (1988:28). The kinds of jobs they were found to undertake are those involving the kind of skills and dispositions that firemen are thought to possess. Driving, usually delivery work (44 per cent), window cleaning (21 per cent) and undertaking (10 per cent) were among the occupations mentioned by Edgell and Hart's sample. What is more, 'it is not uncommon for firemen to take on "fiddle jobs" together or for a fireman to set up a business and "employ" or subcontract work to station colleagues' (1988:32). Only 8.7 per cent of the sample declared any income from outside work and these were those who owned their own small businesses (1988:30).

The term 'fiddle job' is somewhat unfortunate from the point of view of our typology. We have reserved the term 'fiddle' for the category of informal economic activity which relies upon *and* takes place either within, or using the facilities of, the work-place. Whilst the kind of activities described by Edgell and Hart are work-place dependent as far as access to the opportunities are concerned, they do not take place within the work-place, during working hours or with Fire Service equipment (as far as we know!). In the section which follows we will turn to what are, in our scheme of things, *proper* fiddles.

Perks and fiddles: informality on the job

There is nothing necessarily extra-legal about economic activities which lie between work and employment. It is the lack of declaration of income from such activities and the avoidance of employment regulation which determine their extra-legal, specifically informal status. Informality on the job, however, the perks and fiddles described in the work of Ditton (1977), Henry (1978) and Mars and Nicod (1984), for example, and 'the foreigner' or 'the homer', the carrying out of own-account economic activity using the resources of the work-place, are frequently intrinsically extra-legal or illegitimate. We have paid some attention to this kind of economic activity in earlier sections; all we wish to do here is briefly reiterate the more relevant of our earlier observations.

The central feature of these activities from our point of view is not, however, that they are illegal but that they are dependent upon access to regular employment. In a time of high unemployment, such economic activity is, therefore, not a possibility for all people. The difference of opinion between Ditton (1977:173–84) and Henry (1978:15–41) as regards whether there is the potential for fiddling in *all* occupations, or whether it is strictly confined to, or more common in, certain occupations, is also of relevance to the perk and the homer. From our point of view it would appear that certain occupations offer a greater potential for fiddling and perks, and certainly for homers, than others. The potential for such activities cannot, however, be ruled out of *any* employment situation. It depends, rather, upon whether or not there is a demand for the particular commodity or service, whatever it might be, and upon the degree of organizational space available for its provision.

One of the most thoroughgoing considerations of why some work or employment situations are more prone to the practice of fiddling than others is to be found in *Cheats at Work*, by Mars (1982). He suggested that there are five situations in particular which encourage fiddling: where there is an impersonal 'passing trade', with both sides to the transaction usually only meeting once; where expertise can be exploited and the customer is in a position of relative ignorance; where gatekeepers preside over an unbalanced relationship between demand and supply; where there is a triadic relationship between employers, employees and clients and alliances are possible between any two against the third; and where the distribution of effort or skill is varied across an occupation or profession such that there is pressure for economic rewards to be more directly responsive to market conditions than generalized formal pricing allows (Mars, 1982:136–54). Among other things, this formulation is helpful inasmuch as it reminds us that fiddles can be at the expense of the employer, the customer, or both. The five situations are related in that they 'involve the exploitation of a structured imbalance in power between the fiddler and his victim' (1982:154). Four subsidiary factors contributing to 'fiddle-proneness' are identified by Mars (1982:154–9): the existence or effectiveness of control systems, the ambiguities which are attached to certain kinds of goods with respect to values, etc., the ease with which goods can be converted to private use and the anonymity which is a feature of large-scale organizations.

Not only are some situations more likely than others to engender fiddles, but Mars (1982) also argues that different types of occupation involve different types of fiddle. Drawing upon Douglas's framework of 'grid-group analysis' (Douglas, 1973), Mars identifies 'donkey jobs' (involving isolated subordination), 'wolf jobs' (working in packs, or tight work-groups), 'hawk jobs' (characterized by individual entrepreneurial opportunities) and 'vulture jobs' (working in loosely structured work-groups). Each kind of situation, Mars argues, is characterized by distinctive fiddles. Wolf-pack fiddles, for example, involve team work, informal structure and an uneven, hierarchical division of the spoils. Dustcart crews, baggage handlers and dockers may all function as wolf-packs.

The degree to which such activities are formalized also differentiates them. Employer connivance in the perk is not unusual. It is perhaps less conceivable with the fiddle or the homer, although in certain industries recognition, explicit or implicit, of the existence of such practices is common. In some cases, such practices – and the benefits to be derived therefrom – form part of the (explicitly or implicitly) recognized structure of rewards or incentives attached to the job. Providing that the consequences are not defined as serious, as in the example of miners 'picking' coal from company property, they may be tolerated and become legally enforceable 'custom and practice'.

The reasons why employers accept the existence of perks and fiddles are important, and shed light on the nature of these practices. In some cases, their toleration may be a small price to pay for relatively harmonious industrial relations (Mars, 1974).

The 'blind eye' may, what is more, be a useful tactical ace up management's sleeve. It is not, for example, unheard of for employers to ignore systematic small-scale fiddling over a long period of time, until such times as they may wish to be rid of particular individuals or shed a section of the workforce. 'Catching' workers fiddling provides adequate, and legally defensible, public grounds for dismissal. Within limits, therefore, fiddling allows a certain amount of flexibility, at small cost, to be built into the organizational system for the employer. Flexibility and control of the work-place are, in this context, intimately connected.

As we have already suggested, fiddles and perks are also, of course, economic strategies, for both employers and employees. In many low-paid jobs, 'taking a bit off the top' is a necessary financial supplement for workers and an important means by which the employer's costs are kept to a minimum. In this sense, the fiddle may be an invisible component of the wage (Ditton, 1977:86; Mars, 1982:152; South and Scratton, 1981:36–43). There are, what is more, some situations in which employees may actually be formally encouraged to do homers or 'a bit on the side', because the employer participates in the profits. One such case is the university lecturer who engages in consultancy work using university facilities. The employing institution benefits both from overheads payments *and* from the status and symbolic credits which attach to consultancy work in the contemporary moral economy of higher education.

Having so far discussed perks and fiddles as though they were much the same (and, indeed, in many respects they are), it may, finally, be useful to consider the differences between them. Most obviously, perks are more accepted and legitimate than fiddles; there is a general understanding that the latter are illegal. In most cases, however, they are only illegal inasmuch as they are not accepted, whether formally or informally, rather than vice versa. There are grey areas between 'the blind eye' and 'custom and practice', and between the latter and the 'package of benefits' which one sees so often specified in advertisements for management posts, which can be exploited by both sides of the transaction. It is also a question of where one stands. As Mars has observed, *your* fiddles may be *my* perks (1982:3). Similarly, Ditton implies that there may be a class basis to the differentiation – bread salesmen have fiddles, while executives have perks (1977:86, 174–5)–a view with which South and Scratton would seem to agree (1981).

Like homeworking, 'hobbles' and 'doing the double', 'perks', 'fiddles' and 'homers' alert us to the interpenetration of the formal and the informal. More to the point, however, it is possible to argue convincingly that the informal economic activities which we have discussed in this and the previous two sections are actually dependent upon the formal for their existence and continuity. They are in no sense separate from the 'formal sector'. They are, rather, an integral part of the complex network of organizational practices which makes up the mixed economy of social democratic capitalism, sometimes to the extent of state acquiescence or connivance (Portes and Sassen-Koob, 1987; Weiss, 1987). This is not, however, to suggest that they are 'parasitic' upon legitimate business. Quite the reverse: inasmuch as such practices epitomize some of the core values of capitalism, we find it hard to imagine their absence.

Organizing the economy: the informality of formality

In Chapter 1 we argued that the notion of formality was only to be understood in the context of a historical process in which the development of writing and information technology, on the one hand, interacted with the rise of bureaucracy and the modern state, on the other. This is one of the classic central themes of sociology, exemplified most clearly perhaps in the work of Max Weber. To recognize this is to place issues of social control and regulation at the heart of one's understanding of informality.

To look at the first strand of this process, the means by which information is stored and transmitted, the innovation which most obviously created the possibility of formality was writing: 'the technologising of the word' (Ong, 1982). Goody, in an influential series of publications (1977; 1986; 1987) has argued that writing leads to a new way of thinking, a different intellectual framework for the appropriation of the world: generalized rather than contextual, explicit rather than implicit, discontinuous rather than continuous. Literacy allows the storage, manipulation and comparison of information and ideas. What Goody and Ong – whose arguments are in most respects similar – seem to be describing here, in fact, bears a close resemblance to the Weberian notion of formal rationality: 'the degree to which the provision for needs ... is capable of being expressed in numerical, calculable terms, and is so expressed' (Weber, 1978:85). Numeracy and the associated discourse of mathematics are, of course, the most generalized and least contextual forms of literacy (Goody, 1977:122). Literacy and numeracy, therefore, create or encourage monitoring, accounting and economic evaluation. Without these processes, formality is impossible and informality meaningless.

The 'cognitive leap' model of literacy is not unchallenged, however. Street, in particular, argues (1984) that literacy does not have necessary consequences but that the process of literization and formalization must be understood within specific historical and cultural contexts. The power of literacy and numeracy are also bound up with the nature of the technology with which information is stored and transmitted. Febvre and Martin, for example, have documented the impact of printing and 'the coming of the book' on early modern Europe (1976). It should not, however, be thought that successive developments in information technology necessarily entail enhanced formality. In the period since the Second World War, in particular, quantum advances in the nature and power of telecommunications have, in fact, created the possibility of global informal networks. The telephone, in particular, has been influential in enhancing the power of the informal within and between the geographically far-flung organizations of nation states and multi-national economic arenas. The role of a new generation of computer-based information technology, relying neither on the written nor the spoken word, in the definition of the distinction between formality and informality is, as yet, unclear. At least one writer has suggested that modern developments in information technology will lead to a new kind of social solidarity and new forms of the state, based on extended communications networks (Richmond, 1988:173–6).

Bureaucratization and the rise of the state are the other side of the historical process of formalization. The development of literacy, from its earliest forms among the great agrarian civilizations of the Middle East and, later, China, to its subsequent elaboration in Roman and Christian Europe, has always been intimately involved with the needs of the state. These needs, specifically, were in the first instance the codification of custom and dispute procedures and the recording and control of resources, income and tax revenues. In two words, law and accounting. These requirements, which became ever more elaborated with the rise of the modern state, are the basic axes which serve to define formality and informality in the modern world. Formality is the management of affairs according to generalized, explicit rules (Gerth and Mills, 1948:198).

Bureaucracy – whether state, capitalist or whatever – is also about control. If organization theorists and industrial sociologists are agreed on nothing else, they are agreed on this (Blau and Scott, 1963: 165–93; Clegg and Dunkerley, 1980; Salaman, 1979; Simon, 1957:123–53). Control is achieved not merely through rules and accounting procedures, but also in the creation of hierarchical structures of position and status and the limitation of access to information within these structures.

Formality and control within bureaucratic organizations – and this is the other thing upon which students of formal organizations are agreed – are, however, always less than perfect. In the first place, the routine demands of day-to-day interaction, the need to 'get things done', create and encourage informal decision-making and communication networks. Second, just as formality is bound up in *authority*, so *power* may sometimes function best in informal contexts. Third, as Mars has pointed out (1982:157) the very size and formality of large organizations create conditions of possibility and anonymity, economic niches which may be exploited for private, non-organizational ends. Fourth, the pursuit of profit and self-interest frequently entails the evasion of control, whether procedural or financial. Fifth, there are the technical problems attached to size and complexity: not everything can be legislated for, nor can everything be controlled and monitored. Sixth, similarly, not every aspect of organizational life is reducible to economic or quantitative variables; this necessarily renders formalization imperfect and uneven. Finally, it would be unwise to underestimate the obstinate human propensity for resisting control and expanding vast amounts of ingenuity upon 'beating the system' simply for the sake of doing so.

These are among the reasons – given in no necessary order of importance – why informality flourishes within or alongside formality. Both are important within organizations with respect to the exercise and resistance of control. Numerous research studies – of which those cited below are merely examples – attest to the importance of social networks and informal practices within formal bureaucracies: in managerial decision-making (Burns and Stalker, 1961; Gouldner, 1954), in industrial relations (Rose, 1975), in relationships between managers in the 'old boys network' or the 'club' (Fernandez, 1982), in shopfloor or employee relationships (Burawoy, 1979; Turner, 1971) and in selection and recruitment (Jenkins 1986). Neither formality nor informality are absolutes, nor is the relationship between the two necessarily changing or evolving in any predetermined, evolutionary direction, i.e. towards greater formality or 'rationality'. Inasmuch as the key issue is control, levels and varieties of formality and informality will alter as the problem and nature of power and authority shift with the times and the circumstances, although looked at in a longer historical frame of reference, the general trend towards greater formalization is undeniable.

The apparently paradoxical rider which must be added to this conclusion is that, along with greater formality comes, of necessity, increased scope for informality. In a simple sense this is entailed as much by logic as anything else: formality implies its opposite, and vice versa. There is, however, more to it than this. Goody, for example, argues (1987) that the oral or non-literate cultural forms found in a literate social context are qualitatively different from pre-literate cultural forms. More to the point of our discussion is the fact that, economic rationales notwithstanding, it is impossible to offer somebody the symbolic coup of 'something on the side' in the absence of regulation. This is what Henry recognizes – albeit to the unfortunate exclusion of other motivations – in his original analysis of the 'hidden economy' (1978). Neither is it posssible to 'bend the rules' in the absence of rules to bend. The power of formal regulation creates the possibility of its subversion and provides us with a set of attractive social and psychological pay-offs for so doing.

In addition there is the further important point – best exemplified, perhaps, in the complexities of Silverman and Jones's analysis (1976) of United Kingdom civil service selection boards – that the formal is often either an ideal to which aspirations are directed, or a charter which allows for the *ex post-facto* legitimation or interpretation of diverse practice. The formal is not the *actual*, it is simply one element in the social construction of organizational life.

The digression in this section into the issue of the nature of the 'formal' has been a necessarily superficial attempt to compensate for some of the problems or deficiencies, as we see them, of the debate about informal economic activity. There are at least four such shortcomings to which we have implicitly addressed ourselves.

First, there is the reification, or overemphasis, of the formal nature of bureaucratic society, in both the public and private sectors. Not only is the power and scope of formality uneven, but it necessarily implies a thriving informality. Our position here is much the same as Urry's, when he argues that the expansion of the bureaucratic state does not entail the contraction of civil society; in fact, the state and civil society expand side-by-side (1981). This is to do considerable violence to the subtlety of Urry's analysis. The interested reader will find in his discussion a more demanding theoretical framework than we can provide here for the discussion of these issues.

Second, inasmuch as the depiction of any aspect of the economy, or more generally, economic activity, as *either* formal *or* informal is necessarily problematic, the 'separate economies' model is even more suspect than we have elsewhere suggested. This is a further powerful argument for doing away altogether with usages such as 'the informal economy', 'the hidden economy' or 'the black economy'.

Third, our discussion of the relationship between formality and informality, in which we argue that the historical process of formalization necessarily produces a notion of 'informality' and a set of conditions which define it, leads to the conclusion that the informal is both a residual category, i.e. that which is not formally regulated, and a logically structured category in its own right, the meaning of which is only in part determined by the nature of regulation. The formal is simultaneously an absence and a presence within the informal, and vice versa. The double-sided and apparently paradoxical relationship between formality and informality has been overlooked in a literature which has tended to take their meaning largely for granted.

Finally, the arguments which we have rehearsed above suggest that there is no straightforward sense in which informal economic activity can be equated – either explicitly (Henry, 1978:6–11) or implicitly (Pahl, 1984:17–62) – with pre-industrial or pre-capitalist patterns of social life. The informal as we discuss it throughout this book, while it may be an aspect of a continuous and historically deep-seated thread of social practice, is a product of the rise of the bureaucratic, modern state and should be understood as such.

To say this is much the same as saying that deviance is primarily a product of custom and law. In the next section we shall discuss those forms of informal economic activity which have, as their primary social attribute, criminality or deviance.

The wrong side of the law: corruption and crime

Perks, fiddling and the homer may be unlawful or deviant activities, depending on their context. Our final two categories of informal economic activity, corruption and crime, definitely are. For the sake of convenience, we shall discuss them under the same heading here. We categorize these unlawful activities separately, however, because the meanings which are attached to such activities by participants and observers are not homogeneous. We differentiate, in so doing, between degrees of seriousness and immorality as commonsensically perceived. It would, for example, be inappropriate to deal with the use of a photocopying machine belonging to an employer for one's private purposes (a perk or a fiddle), in the same way as the sale of heroin (crime), or the acceptance of a bribe to favour a particular tender for work (corruption). It is this latter situation, corruption, which we address first, concluding the section with a discussion of our final category, crime.

First, however, a brief explanation of our somewhat unorthodox approach to illegal economic activity. Most criminology and the sociology of deviance addresses itself – in reflection perhaps of the functioning of the state legal system – to working-class crime. We have attempted to move away from this concentration, redressing the balance by looking in particular at white-collar crime, although not to the exclusion of other illegal activities. As subject-matter, white-collar crime permits us to make the points which we are seeking to emphasize, while illustrating the widespread distribution through the social structure of the general category 'illegal economic activity'. Furthermore, in discussing practices such as fiddling and homers in previous sections, we have already referred to a considerable amount of material relating to 'blue-collar crime' of one sort or another.

Finally, inasmuch as white-collar crime is in general clearly identified with business activity, its status as economic activity is as unambiguous as one can reasonably hope for. This, however, is an issue to which we shall return at the end of this section.

To turn first to corruption, Doig points out that in medieval politics 'private benefit from and through the holding of office and the exercise of the vote was acceptable and universal practice' (1984:27). The development of what are now regarded as acceptable standards of behaviour in public life has been the result of legislation during succeeding centuries, part of the historical process of formalization and state formation which we discussed above. The increasing democratization of society was dependent upon, and stimulated by, this process (Dearlove and Saunders, 1984:17–25). Private benefit from and through the holding of office is not today regarded as publicly acceptable behaviour in the United Kingdom or elsewhere. Even in medieval times bribery as such was an offence both in statute and common law; it was not, however, legislated against in its current form in the United Kingdom until the end of the nineteenth century. Corruption in the medieval polity was understood as the *excessive* or *arbitrary* use of power for selfish means. It was a matter of degree. In the western social democracies today, legislation governs both the state and civil society in this respect and serves to add legitimacy to the operation of public and private institutions. Such developments have not, however, eradicated the misuse of power by those in public employment or authority, as is comprehensively illustrated by Doig's survey of the United Kingdom since the Second World War (1984). Nor is there any reason to believe that Britain is a particularly severe case; the reverse, in fact, may be true.

Corruption is described by Bequai (1978b) as 'bribes, kickbacks and political frauds' in his chapter on the subject. He sees the category as including four types of activity. First, there is private corruption which, for example, might involve the bribing of one commercial firm or organization by another in order to encourage the use of its services. This may be in contravention of government regulations relating to fair trading and competition. Second, there is bureaucratic bribery. Here members of a civil service might avail themselves of inducements to provide information or services to others. Third, there is political bribery. This can take place in the international arena but, with the increasing importance of local government, is perhaps more likely to occur within state boundaries. It might, for example, take the form of the granting of permission to proceed with a particular activity which requires local authority sanction. Finally, Bequai includes electioneering fraud, either by political party workers registering unqualified voters, falsifying records or intimidating election officials, for example, or by election officers falsifying electoral records. Different kinds of corruption are regulated in different ways. For example, to use Bequai's classification, private corruption tends to be less within the ambit of the law than, say, political corruption.

Corruption may be regarded as one area of what is referred to as 'white-collar crime' (Sutherland, 1949), itself a part of that range of behaviour that is labelled 'criminal'. The Chamber of Commerce of the United States has defined white-collar crime as, 'any illegal act characterized by deceit and concealment and not dependent on the direct application of physical force' (1974:6). Sutherland's work on nominally criminal behaviour which was not normally subject to the attention of criminologists provided an important addition to the traditional criminological research agenda. Much criminal behaviour, for example, had been explained as the outgrowth of 'cultures of poverty' (Merton, 1957:144–7; Miller, 1958). Even the highly organized crime syndicate could have its origins explained in this way. However, the recognition of criminal activity among the apparently 'respectable' echelons of society required different causal explanations of crime from those which are dependent upon material deprivation. Those who are already financially well-off cannot have their participation in criminal activity explained purely in terms of the need to survive. Some criminal activity may be interpreted as a challenge or a game (Miller, 1958; Walsh, 1981); in other situations it is tantamount to running a business (McIntosh, 1975). Other 'criminals' may engage in such activities for political reasons. These are but some of the possible motives. By way of an example, we shall explore motivation, among other considerations, in the context of a particularly topical form of white-collar crime: computer fraud.

Bequai reports that computer crime contributes substantially to the total of white-collar crime in the United States. It is estimated to have amounted to $100 million annual turnover at the time he was writing (Bequai, 1978a:1). From the participant's point of view it is an attractive form of activity because detection is rare. Even where computer fraud is detected there is a marked reluctance on the part of organizations to bring it to the attention of the authorities because of the damage which such revelations might do to public confidence in the enterprise. In those instances where a prosecution is brought, the punishment is unlikely to be in keeping with the seriousness of the crime measured in monetary terms. The perpetrators of such acts are likely to be treated leniently by the courts.

Bequai isolates the potential 'types' of computer felon: 'Some steal for personal gain, others for the challenge, and still others because they are pawns in a larger scheme' (1978a:4). The first type of person conforms to the 'relative material deprivation' explanation of crime; the other two would not, however. Other motives for participation in this form of activity are operative here. Bequai is particularly interested in the degree to which criminal syndicates are becoming involved in computer crime. He sees this as a new and worrying development which, as yet, has gone unstudied (although, see Yeager, 1976, for a discussion of organized crime as white-collar crime).

What is particularly interesting about Bequai's work on computer fraud is his analysis of social attitudes to the seriousness of computer crime as manifest in the sentencing practices of the courts in relation to those convicted of white-collar crimes generally. While this is an American study there is no reason to believe that similar attitudes do not pertain in the United Kingdom. In a study of white-collar criminals, Bequai (1978a:5–6) found that 26 per cent of his sample, who each stole an average of $21.6 million, received only fines, suspended sentences or probation; 16.7 per cent, who stole an average of $23.6 million, received sentences of one year or less; while only 30 per cent, stealing on average $16 million each, received prison sentences of up to three years. Whatever else was being used to assess the seriousness of the crime it clearly was not the amount of money involved in the fraud.

While we do not wish to suggest that, as Bequai would have it, harsher sentencing practices for white-collar criminals would act as a deterrent and thus reduce the incidence of such criminal behaviour, it does appear that the pattern of sentencing described above appears to reflect a more lenient attitude taken towards white-collar crime than towards other forms of crime. It is tempting to explain such practices as a manifestation of class bias. Sutherland (1949:3) established a general correspondence between white-collar crime and higher social class membership. Those areas of criminal activity common to the working class which, according to the US Chamber of Commerce definition mentioned above, would count as white-collar crime – in particular, social security fraud – arouse public condemnation and harsh treatment in the courts out of all proportion to the financial seriousness of the offences (Golding and Middleton, 1978; 1982). There are clear empirical grounds for positing a relationship between the crimes of the working class and the harshness of sentencing, particularly as measured by the incidence of the use of incarceration (Box, 1981:191–6).

This observation adds a new dimension to the argument that opportunities for participation in various forms of informal economic activity, and the benefits to be derived therefrom, are not equally accessible to all members of society. Nor, needless to say, are either the likelihood of apprehension attaching to illegal economic activities, or the penalties attaching to apprehension and conviction, equally distributed. The consequences of participation in particular forms of criminal informal economic activity vary inasmuch as different types of criminal behaviour, varying in degree of public condemnation, are characteristic – for whatever reasons – of different classes within society. For all forms of economic activity, differing opportunity structures exist in reflection of differing positions in the stratification system. Crime is no exception.

We have discussed social attitudes to crime and the participants' motives for engaging in such activity. We shall finally consider in greater detail the channels of access to opportunities for crime and for the distribution of the produce of crime. It has been a central argument throughout this book that the ability to participate in many types of informal economic activity is contingent upon the existence of, and access to, social networks. To illustrate this point, we can look at different forms of criminal activity. Computer fraud is insufficiently researched to allow us to use it as the medium for this exploration, so we must spread our net further afield.

At one level, everybody has the potential to engage in criminal activity of one sort or another. Anybody can go into a shop and take goods without paying for them. Such activity could be described, without too much irony, as self-provisioning through crime. The participant, or the participant's household, either consumes the product directly or uses the product stolen to provide themselves with final services. However, if we consider criminal activity of a non-individual nature, where the product of the work is not easily transformed for consumption purposes, the need to study the social contacts required for entry into these more complex criminal activities, and for the distribution or conversion of the product of those activities, becomes more apparent.

One major criminological understanding of opportunities for criminal activity is represented by 'ecological' studies of crime. Shaw and McKay's (1969) pioneering work in Chicago during the 1920s included a survey of the geographical distribution of crime which they discovered was closely related to the existence of 'criminal areas' in the large cities. While individual motivations mediated the effects of the local environment, local conditions appeared to influence heavily the propensity to engage in criminal activity. This approach remains influential today and accounts for much policing policy (although it must be added, of course, that policing policy is an extremely influential determinant of the distribution of recorded crime). Opportunities to participate in financially rewarding criminal activity come through contact with those who themselves are involved in criminal activity. Shaw and McKay, and other sociologists and criminologists subsequently adopting or criticizing the ecological approach to the study of crime (i.e. Gill, 1977; Morris, 1957; Parker, 1974; Reynolds, 1986; Suttles, 1968), have concentrated on the geographical proximity of criminals. Often such geographical concentration has been associated – both in the public eye and in the eyes of researchers – with immigrant communities, for example, Afro-Caribbeans in Britain (Pryce, 1979), the Italians in the United States (Nelli, 1976) or Surinamers in Amsterdam (Punch, 1979).

While there can be no doubt that, certainly in the first instance, geographical concentration played a major role in the rise and continuity of networks of organized criminal economic activity, it should also be recognized that social networks other than those dependent upon geographical proximity may also be important. A professional or occupational network might, for example, be just as useful. We would suspect that this is particularly true with respect to computer fraud or other kinds of white-collar crime. Such networks may, particularly with the expansion and sophistication of telecommunications, be international, if not – in the wake of the revolutionary changes in the financial and stock markets in 1986 – global.

We turn finally to the distribution of the proceeds of criminal activity. Cash proceeds are easily distributed. Some products of crime, however, need to be converted for the personal use of those participating. The 'fence' has long been regarded as the crucial link in this process. For Klockars (1974:172), the 'fence' is a dealer in stolen property, the middleman between the sellers (thieves) and the buyers (receivers) of stolen goods, who regularly buys and sells without detection by the authorities and has a public reputation for so doing. The management of the contradiction between carrying out clandestine activities while maintaining a public reputation for so doing is a major part of the art of the fence.

The fence represents the specialization of an activity which can be carried out by thieves themselves but there are risks involved and these can be avoided or reduced by using the services of someone skilled at distributing stolen goods. The distribution of the proceeds of criminal activity is necessarily risky for the thief, however undertaken. Fences themselves may be a security hazard. In their study of burglars, for example, Bennett and Wright note that:

> Other offenders were informed on not by their colleagues, but by the person to whom they had sold the stolen goods. This often happened after a 'fence' had been arrested and (presumably to improve his own position) had revealed the names of the offenders from whom he had bought the goods.
> (1984:120)

The opportunities for, and the benefits to be derived from, criminal activity do not, then, appear to be equally available to all. Social networks are necessary both to make the relevant contacts for the more remunerative forms of criminal activity, and to minimize the risks which are inherent in such work. Of all the forms of 'shady' informal activity which we have discussed, those which are legally defined as criminal in themselves carry the greatest risk of detection and prosecution.

As we indicated at the beginning of this section, ours has been an idiosyncratic discussion of criminal economic activity. It has also, for reasons of space, been superficial. In closing, there are a number of general points about the broad topic which are worthy of emphasis.

In the first place, as with so many of our categories of informal economic activity, there is no hard boundary surrounding either 'crime' or 'corruption'. They overlap each other and tail off into other areas, most obviously the fiddles, perks and homers of 'informality on the job'.

This indeterminacy is related to one of the central characteristics of crime: the nature of deviance is socially defined and crime, in particular, is defined by reference to a codified body of law and custom. There is no such thing as a specific criminal activity *sui generis*; not even homicide is so defined. The social definition of what constitutes criminal economic activity, therefore, varies with historical, cultural and social context. This – which is no more than a summation of labelling theory (Schur, 1971; Lemert, 1972) – is a more specific version of the general proposition outlined in the previous section. Just as the informal is created by formal regulation, so is the criminal created by the law and its enforcement. However, to follow further our earlier argument concerning informality, the criminal is not merely a residual category, the meaning of which is solely defined in opposition to the 'good' or the legitimate. It has also meaning and a logical structure which are produced by criminals themselves in the pursuit of their deviant business and social activities (Becker, 1963).

With reference to the relationship between the formal and the informal, criminal economic activity illustrates clearly the close and ill-defined relationship between the two. This is most apparent in the case of organized crime (McIntosh, 1975), one of the most comprehensively documented branches of which is the Italian-American network often referred to as the 'Mafia' (Arlacchi, 1986; Blok, 1974; Hess, 1973; Ianni and Reuss-Ianni, 1972; Pantaleone, 1966). There are two key issues here. The first is the need to transform the cash generated by illegitimate business and crime into legitimate funds, which can then be set to work in the investment and other markets of the 'overground' economy. Money in the amounts which we are here considering must, in the context of the modern state, be accounted for before it can be spent. This involves the 'laundering' procedures discussed in Chapter 5. The second problem is the need to maintain an accommodation between large and frequently highly visible criminal businesses – everything from the production and marketing of drugs, to organized prostitution, to illegal gambling – and the control apparatus of the state. This, of necessity, involves political and bureaucratic corruption (Ianni and Reuss-Ianni, 1976; Pantaleone, 1966). In the case of both issues, we find a subtle and complicated articulation between the formal/legitimate and the informal/criminal.

Similarly, our brief discussion of the motives for criminal economic activity illustrates the difficulty in clearly establishing a category of the 'economic'. People engage in criminal economic activity for a variety of reasons in addition to the central pursuit of material advantage: the quest for influence, excitement, identity, or whatever. The case of criminal 'big business', particularly in its close relationship with politics – a relationship which may not be too dissimilar to the relationship existing between politics and legitimate business – is a further justification for scepticism concerning the possibility of delineating the 'economic' as a domain of discourse and practice in its own right. We shall return to this important question in Chapter 8.

Finally, and this once again is to reiterate a general theme of our discussion so far, access to criminal economic activity is not uniform. It is determined by an opportunity structure which is directly related to class position and formal employment status, on the one hand, and the communal and cultural barriers to participation in the appropriate informal social networks, on the other. It is also, although we have not explored the matter here, structured by gender roles and the gendered division of criminal labour, which define what kinds of criminal careers are open to women – typically either prostitution or various peripheral 'service' jobs – and in what capacity – typically as subordinates, not 'bosses'. In these three senses, criminal informal activity is organized on much the same lines as other kinds of economic activity, whether formal or informal.

The varieties of informal economic activity

In this chapter we have discussed a variety of categories of informal economic activity, ranging from self-employment to voluntary work to crime. Within these categories, we have drawn upon a diversity of published research evidence to illustrate the spectrum of practices which may be included under any particular heading. There are a number of general themes which emerge from our discussion.

It is clear, for example, that although the nine categories which we have used to structure our discussion of the literature are useful for the organization and comparison of data, the boundaries between them are less than water-tight. In particular cases there is uncertainty about how an activity should be most aptly categorized. Activities may be moved between categories, depending on their historical and social context. This is no more than one might expect; the analytical scheme which we have outlined in this chapter is designed to be flexible in the face of the complexities and heterogeneities of the 'real world'. Inasmuch as our analysis is grounded in, and generated by, a theoretically conditioned engagement with those complexities, the 'real world' is, in fact, the source of our categories. As we explained at the beginning of the book, however, we are confining our attention to a particular kind of social reality, the social democracies of Western capitalism. A different type of social situation – a state socialist economy, for example – would produce a different model, composed of different categories.

Staying with the issue of the definition of categorical boundaries, we have drawn attention in this chapter to the problems inherent in attempting to maintain a firm distinction between the formal and the informal. At the empirical level, if no other, this is not straightforward: the formal and the informal are typically present to some degree in all social situations in the societies which we have been discussing. There is a considerable amount of interpenetration of the one with the other. What is more, inasmuch as the definition of the formal is historically specific, contingent upon the legal and bureaucratic rules and frameworks characterizing any particular situation, the nature of the formal – and the informal – shifts with the context.

Viewed in this way, informality becomes nothing more than a category of residual identification: the informal is simply that which is not formal. While this is true, it is also a somewhat simple-minded conceptualization of the situation. As we have argued in this chapter, informality is not merely the absence of formal regulation (although without such regulation there could be no such thing as informality). Informality is a social condition in its own right, with its own rules, conditions and characteristic modes of representation. An appreciation of the dual nature of informality – as both a residual category *and* in itself a framework of social experience – is missing from the bulk of the literature on the topic.

One of the most important examples of the interpenetration of formality and informality is to be found in the relationship between informal economic activity and the formal labour market. Aspects of the latter are in many senses dependent upon varieties of the former. We have argued this point in our discussions of homeworking, women's domestic work, 'women's work', the area which lies between work and employment, fiddles and perks, and bureaucratic organizations. We do not think it requires further expansion here.

All the conclusions which we have so far summarized provide further support for one of the most basic strands in our argument. We can find no defensible reason for continuing to talk about separate economies, be they 'hidden', 'black', 'underground', 'informal' or whatever. Empirically, such notions are inaccurate. Theoretically speaking, they serve to divert attention away from the complexity of the historical relationships between various kinds of economic activity. In terms of research practice, their effect has been to encourage the futile expenditure of effort upon the quest for chimera (most typically, some version of the 'value' of the 'informal economy'). In the discourse of politicians and civil servants, notions of a separate economy are used to disguise real social problems, to tinker with unemployment statistics and to legitimate punitive welfare policies. Such dubious political objectives aside, it is difficult to imagine what, if anything, the separate economies model has left to commend it.

Accepting, however, that there is a range of economic activity which may be identified as more or less informal, it is overwhelmingly clear from the literature that access to opportunities for informal economic activity is not uniformly distributed throughout the population. The unemployed, for example, typically have fewer opportunities in this respect than the employed. Influential factors impinging upon informal economic opportunities, affecting both the nature and scale of their availability, include gender, locality, ethnicity, employment status, occupation and age. Of these, the discussion in this chapter suggests that gender and employment status may be the most significant (Hoyman, 1987; Pahl, 1987).

Finally, it is important to remember that informal economic activity should be seen in its proper historical context, specifically the rise of the modern bureaucratic state and the development of writing and information technology. To acknowledge this is to place the public and private control of economic life, through the impositions of power and the exercise of authority, at the centre of our analytical framework. To return briefly to the arguments of Chapters 1 and 2, the distinction between 'work' and 'employment', itself the product of an historical process of capitalist development, is also crucial in placing our subject-matter in its proper social setting. Neither formality nor informality should be taken for granted. It is one of the weaknesses of the literature in this area that questions about the status and meaning of formality and informality are largely left unasked, let alone answered.

In a number of places in this chapter we have raised the question of the distinction between the economic and the non-economic. This distinction is as important as the contrast between formality and informality as a defining criterion of our subject area. It is just as frequently problematic. The difference between certain kinds of informal economic activity and leisure pursuits, for example, is often far from clear-cut. We shall discuss this topic in more detail in the next chapter.

Chapter 8

LEISURE AND SOCIAL OBLIGATIONS

In Chapter 2 we defined, for the purposes of our discussion, the terms 'work' and 'employment'. While recognizing that work is not limited to the field of employment, we also argued that a distinction of some kind is necessary between 'work outside employment' and other social activity. We expressly introduced the term 'economic activity' to differentiate both employment and work from other aspects of social life. We did not, at that stage, however, touch upon the question of the nature of these other social activities. In this chapter we shall do so with specific reference to leisure, which is, perhaps, the archetypal non-work activity.

We are concerned in the first part of this chapter with the attempt by Hoggett and Bishop (1985) to conceptualize the voluntary organization of leisure opportunities in terms of an informal economy model. Their approach has the usual characteristics of the informal economy literature: the subject-matter is arbitrarily chosen and unnecessarily narrow, there is much terminological confusion and the work contains that perennial favourite, an attempt to quantify the value of informal economic activity. We try to come to terms with this muddle through a discussion of other sociological work on leisure, in particular the work of Parker (1983). In the second part of this chapter, we develop Parker's categories, to render them compatible with our own framework for understanding the formality and informality of economic activity. This framework is extended to include non-economic, or social, activities such as

leisure pursuits. Finally, we briefly discuss the literture dealing
with the 'post-industrial' or 'leisure society'.

Defining leisure: some difficulties

Although the 'informal economy' is not the major concern of
Hoggett and Bishop's study, they conclude their discussion of
'patterns of mutual aid in leisure' with an attempt to
conceptualize the organization of communal leisure activities in
terms of an informal economy model. While acknowledging that
certain leisure activities generate a product which is marketable
in the formal or informal (black) economies, or barterable in the
informal (household) economy, they are more interested in the
production of leisure opportunities than the products of leisure.
We shall concentrate here upon what they have to say about the
production of such opportunities and its relation to the hidden or
informal economy.

Hoggett and Bishop suggest that the voluntary organization of
'communal leisure group activities', such as amateur dramatics
and football, through clubs, associations, societies and the like, is
'an element of what Gershuny would call "the informal
communal economy"' (1985:125). They concentrate on such
activities in order to move away from a dominant view of leisure
which, in equating it with relatively passive consumption, tends,
they suggest, to demean it. For example, Gorz has argued (1965)
that just as the capitalist system shapes a person's working day,
so it also shapes his or her leisure activities: the system 'tells'
people what to consume as leisure. Similarly, Marcuse (1968:
21-2) talks of the creation of 'false needs' in relation to the
consumption of leisure activities. The organization of leisure
activity is seen by Hoggett and Bishop as the productive side of
leisure. It is, 'activity which is freely given yet typically assumes
the form of highly skilled and imaginative work while remaining
leisure and not employment' (Hoggett and Bishop, 1985:1).
However, although Gershuny (1983) notes a tendency for
productive activity generally to move from the formal to the
informal sphere, Hoggett and Bishop, in this particular instance,
detect a tendency in the opposite direction. They talk about 'state
colonialism' and 'the commercialization and commodification of
communal leisure', that is a movement of the production of
leisure opportunities from the informal to the formal sphere,
from civil society to the state.

Hoggett and Bishop regret this trend towards the bureaucratization of leisure. The increasing formalization of the organization of communal leisure activity is described as a threat to the independence, and even the existence, of groups of enthusiasts. Leisure professionals are said to perceive a 'voluntary sector' in leisure, a notion which is apparently 'bizarre' to those who presently organize and participate in activities such as angling and drama, as well as to Hoggett and Bishop themselves. Leisure professionals, it is argued, see the voluntary sector as existing to fill the gaps in statutory provision and as itself amenable to management and manipulation.

It is this approach on the part of the emergent leisure profession which prompts Hoggett and Bishop to estimate the possible market value of voluntary sector activities in leisure. They speculate, for example, as to the actual cost to Leicester City Council of organizing all the amateur football in the area should it become a public sector responsibility (Hoggett and Bishop, 1985:125). They begin their calculations by assuming that the chairman, secretary, treasurer and manager at each club together put in eight hours work per week. They then estimate the cost of the number of extra council employees which would have to be recruited to sustain the 200 or so teams in the area. They come to a figure of £1 million and this, they point out, is without taking account of the fact that teams provide their own kit, balls, goal posts and even pavilions and pitches in some cases. All this effort is conceptualized as part of Britain's hidden economy. As Pahl has observed, in a review of Hoggett and Bishop's work, by putting

> market values on the activities of all those doing basketball, aerobics, lapidary, skittles, orienteering, silk-screen printing, mouse-fancying, leek growing, aero-modelling and scores of others...we could increase our GDP by 40 per cent or whatever.
>
> (Pahl, 1986:30)

There does indeed seem to be something seriously awry with the notion that those who engage in the voluntary organization of communal leisure activities are participating in an activity which has a market value. From Hoggett and Bishop's perspective it would appear that any and every activity conceivable could be allocated a market value.

And, indeed, it has to be admitted that there is no activity or item which does not *in theory* command a market value. Elementary economics insists that this is so. It is equally elementary, however, that it is only so – and forgive the statement of the obvious – if there is actually a market for that service or product. In other words, if there is a relationship between supply and demand which is mediated through some kind of pricing mechanism. Markets do not exist naturally nor can their logic simply be arbitrarily imposed on a particular situation: markets either emerge over a long period of time as a result of a process of historic development, or they have to be made. If they do not actually exist, however, it makes no sense to infer or estimate the market value of a given item or activity. In the absence of a functioning market there can be no such thing as a market value, notional or otherwise. This is the key conceptual error which lies at the heart of many attempts to quantify the value of particular forms of informal economic activity. We will return to this point later.

A second error, less critical in its effects but nonetheless of importance, concerns the differing nature of things which can be bought and things which cannot. The point in this context is that, were, for example, a local authority to provide professional organizers to run local leisure-time activities in the manner suggested by Hoggett and Bishop, it would not be the same kind of organization. Work done on the voluntary basis, for no financial reward, is embedded in a different set of social networks, responds to different values, can mobilize a different set of rewards, penalties, resources and pressures, and involves a different orientation to the allocation of time than paid work (particularly paid work in employment). The two things are qualitatively different and no easy equation between them – whether in terms of notional financial values or otherwise – is possible.

Before we develop our criticism of Hoggett and Bishop's use of an informal economy model in the context of a discussion of leisure, we need to be clear about the sense in which they use the term. 'Leisure' is a notoriously difficult term to define. Their subject matter is clearly only a part of what we could, in the widest definition, regard as leisure: 'communal leisure group activities'. They do not address individual self-provisioning in leisure, for example, although presumably they would not deny that this exists. We have already referred to their characterization of the specific activities upon which they have decided to focus. We shall now look further at their analysis in order to understand better the view of leisure they are proposing.

First, they describe the *conditions* under which leisure activity is undertaken: it is 'activity which is freely given'. In other words the activity is undertaken voluntarily. There is no coercion. Second, they refer to the *kind* of activity concerned. It is 'highly skilled and imaginative work' and hence no different from that which might be expected in many employment situations. However, third and last, they emphasize what it is not. It is not employment.

Parker has observed that definitions of leisure fall into three broad categories (1983:3–7). First, there are 'residual'-type definitions, which focus on the time aspect. Leisure is seen as that period after work and other obligations have been met. Leisure time is, 'roughly equivalent to free time, that time left over after meeting commitments to work and such essential human maintenance as sleeping, eating and personal hygiene' (Vickerman, 1980:192). Second, there are those definitions which build upon the 'residual' approach by introducing a consideration of the quality of leisure activity in addition to its temporal dimension. Such approaches contrast the experience of leisure activity with the experience of work. They tend to stress the significance of 'discretion' or 'choice' in the use of leisure-time. Third, there are those definitions which concentrate solely on the qualitative aspects of leisure activity. Dumazedier (1960:527) stresses that, in order to be called leisure, an activity must both be time free from obligations and function so as to enhance relaxation or community participation. In all three types of definition, Parker discerns a tendency to allocate time and/or activity to the domain of work *or* the domain of leisure. He argues that to do either is a gross oversimplification.

As we have seen, Hoggett and Bishop do admit the possibility of work (albeit highly skilled and imaginative) in leisure. However, it is clear that they do not use the term work in the same manner as Parker. They define the notion in such a way as to make it virtually indistinguishable from any other kind of social activity. In earlier chapters we have already discussed the problematic nature of such a broad definition. However, it is equally clear that Parker's notion of work differs from the definition which we offer in Chapter 2. He uses the term work to refer mainly to employment, although he is, unfortunately, not specific about this (1983:1–3). Hoggett and Bishop distinguish primarily between leisure and employment; in doing so they lay themselves open to Parker's criticism concerning the over-simplification attendant upon identifying certain periods of time with a certain quality of activity. In the discussion which follows we depart, on occasions, from our own distinction between work and employment. This is necessary in order to remain within the framework set by Parker and Hoggett and Bishop.

Hoggett and Bishop also argue that leisure involves an activity which is freely given. Fagin has observed that, 'the concept of control seems to be psychologically crucial when one is looking at the distinction between work and leisure' (1979:35). Parker makes much of this characteristic of leisure activity when introducing a 'time scheme' for the analysis of 'life space'; a life space equals the sum total of a person's activities and ways of spending their time (Parker, 1983:7). While time is broken down into 'work' and 'non-work', the activity which is denoted as leisure is not merely equated with 'non-work time' but is one of three sub-divisions of non-work time. This type of conceptualization is particularly helpful because it allows us to describe the activities of groups such as the retired or the unemployed, for example, as something other than leisure. The important variable in terms of the quality of the activity is 'the extent to which the activity is constrained or freely chosen' (Parker,1983: 10). Clearly the majority of either the retired or the unemployed cannot be described as having *chosen* their lifestyle. Economic and social factors which are largely outside their control have determined their position.

Parker's conceptualization of the relationship between time and activity takes the form – as we have already mentioned – of a distinction between work and non-work, while activities are categorized on a continuum from 'constraint' to 'freedom' (1983:10). He identifies six categories of activity, three each within work and non-work time. In the context of work, he suggests a sequence between constraint and freedom comprised of work (employment), work obligations, and 'leisure in work'. In non-work time the equivalent sequence is made up of the meeting of physiological needs, non-work obligations and leisure activities.

It will be noted that in his scheme, leisure is not only a sub-division of non-work time, but may also be identified within work time. While, as noted above, freedom of choice is a key aspect of leisure activity in this model, there is no necessary restriction of this quality to non-working time. Leisure activity may take place within the context of work. This may, what is more, be communal and, if so, may require organization. ' "Work" and "leisure in work" may (even) consist of the same activity; the difference is that the latter is chosen for its own sake' (Parker, 1983:11). Parker is here pointing out that not all time *in* work is spent *at* work. Equipped with these observations we can return to our critique of Hoggett and Bishop's study.

There are four points within Parker's 'two-dimensional time and activity scheme' where the organization of communal leisure group activities might be located. In only two instances, however, 'leisure' and 'leisure in work', could such organization be described as voluntary and, therefore, count in this context as production in leisure. As Hoggett and Bishop themselves emphasize (1985:123), leisure activity has, by their definition, to be voluntary. What, however, of Parker's categories 'work obligations' and 'non-work obligations'?

First, the production or organization of communal leisure group activities constitutes work (employment) where such production is undertaken by the public or private sector. It is very definitely not a leisure activity for those who undertake it. Second, such organization may take place within the hours of work (employment) yet not, in fact, be work. Wadel points out, for example, that, 'Business organisations are likely to define work as those activities which they find necessary for whatever production is involved. Activities during "working time" which cannot be so related are generally not termed work: they are "leisure at work" or informal activity' (1979:367). Although the voluntary organization of communal leisure group activities such as the card school at work is definitely – within our scheme of things – a leisure activity, such activity is apparently not considered to be so by Hoggett and Bishop.

Finally, there is the organization of leisure activities under the heading of 'non-work obligations'. Here the activity is under-taken as a result of expectations emanating from some non-work relationship. There is a considerable overlap here with our categories of 'household' and 'communal' informal economic activity, discussed in some detail in Chapter 7. We are thinking here, for example, of the mother who organizes a BMX league because her children and their friends have no outlet for their enthusiasm. In undertaking to organize the league she is discharging a parental duty and, possibly, entering into a network of communal reciprocity. Were her children not BMX enthusiasts it would never have occurred to her to engage in such activity. She may enjoy her organizational role, but her time is not freely given in the sense which we understand is required for it to be defined by Hoggett and Bishop or Parker as leisure. Such organization can only constitute leisure – so defined – where the organizing activity itself has the quality of time freely given by the person concerned. To use Hoggett and Bishop's terminology, the *producer* needs also to be a *consumer* for the organization of communal leisure group activities to be regarded as in itself leisure. This may be illustrated with reference to the fourth point in Parker's scheme where such activity may be found, within 'leisure' itself. The railway enthusiast who organizes a trip by rail to a narrow gauge railway could be said to be involved in leisure while actually planning the trip. Consulting timetables and scheduling departure times and connections is likely to be an integral part of the leisure activity for him. The activity is time freely given and as such it counts as production in leisure.

Now it must be acknowledged that the distinction between the last two categories in Parker's scheme, i.e. 'non-work obligations' and 'leisure', may easily become blurred. For example, we might envisage a situation where, although an organizational responsibility was originally taken on by someone voluntarily, without coercion, through time others have come to rely on the organizational skills of that individual, who then feels obliged to continue in the organizational role even though the activity has become an encumberance and a positive barrier to personal leisure. It would seem that while account must be taken of the actors' perceptions of what they are doing and the social relationships involved in any activity, these perceptions and relationships may change over time, thus altering the character of the particular organizational activity from leisure to something else, for example, a non-work obligation.

There are thus two sets of semantic oppositions bound up in the definition of leisure – freedom/choice: obligation, and the economic: the non-economic. In each case, the relationship between the opposing categories is not straightforward. The second opposition, relating to how one defines the economic, is discussed in the following section. The question of the nature of choice and the meaning of obligation is, however, an ancient, and possibly irresolvable, philosophical debate which we do not propose to enter. Concepts such as 'the will', 'voluntarism', 'intention' and 'choice' are so slippery that we do not wish to lose our footing by treading a path among them. Suffice it to say that the reader should remain aware – even if Parker or Hoggett and Bishop are not – of the considerable difficulties involved in using the distinction between choice and obligation as a criterion for defining leisure. This is all the more so given that, as we have discussed in earlier chapters, the capitalist labour market and the wage labour relationship is predicated upon the notional 'freedom' of labour.

Leisure and informal economic activity

Drawing on Parker's work, we have argued that it is an over-simplification to regard all non-work organization of communal leisure group activity as 'voluntary'. We have identified periods outside of work time when such activity is undertaken non-voluntarily, that is as the result of non-work obligations. We have also suggested that the character of an activity may change over time. How can one relate these observations to Hoggett and Bishop's argument that the unpaid organization of communal leisure has the status of informal economic activity? In the first instance, we can only proceed by clarifying some of the terms and categories used by Hoggett and Bishop, and also Parker, in order to make them compatible with our own terminology, as outlined in Chapter 2, and the framework for conceptualizing the relationship between formality and informality which we introduced in Chapter 4.

We have alluded to three different usages of the term 'work' in relation to 'leisure': Hoggett and Bishop's, Parker's and our own. While Hoggett and Bishop's usage is much too wide (it does not distinguish between work and any other social activity), Parker's usage is too narrow (work is synonymous with employment). The definition of work which we outlined in Chapter 2 distinguishes it from other social activity, on the one hand, and employment, on the other. We adopted the term 'economic activity' to cover both work and employment. The distinction between work and employment is particularly important in discussing leisure: while leisure within employment is conceivable, leisure within some kinds of work outside employment is less so. For example, the self-employed, inasmuch as they do not sell their time, are typically either working or not.

Because of this problem with Parker's use of the term work, his distinction between work and non-work must be rejected as unhelpful. For example, the meeting of physiological needs, which he regards as a non-work activity, would, according to our approach, in certain forms constitute work. Many domestic tasks, for example, are conceptualized as work within our framework.

We prefer, therefore, to introduce our distinction between economic and non-economic activities in the place of Parker's distinction between work and non-work. We do not, however, think that it is either sensible or possible to specify in 'objective' or context-free terms what either kind of activity actually is, except in the broadest possible manner. In any given cultural context it will be commonsensically apparent that certain activities are unambiguously economic in their nature (or not, as the case may be). In the case of many other activities, however, it is likely to be less clear-cut. In this sense, the 'science' of economics should be viewed as a particular cultural framework for understanding the world, albeit one which, for historical reasons, has achieved an unusually global degree of dominance.

In keeping with this general approach, therefore, we conceive of a continuum from the economic to the non-economic in any given social situation along which particular activities may move according to varying circumstances. The organization of communal leisure group activities may, as we have shown, be an economic activity. However, in other contexts it may also be a non-economic activity. As a result of our deliberate avoidance of a rigid a priori distinction between the economic and the non-economic, we suggest that obligations which arise out of the work (employment) situation and those which arise out of the non-work situation have so much in common that they should not be distinguished too sharply. They are situated close together on the continuum between economic and non-economic activity. We are equally unhappy with the notion that control over one's activity or, at least, the absence of constraint, is the characteristic feature of leisure activity. The self-employed, for example, clearly have a great degree of control over what they do, yet their activity is not leisure. On the other hand, leisure activities may be pursued or organized as the meeting of powerful social obligations. Parker's freedom-constraint perspective is, therefore, omitted from our framework.

Instead, we return to the distinction between formality and informality. We have already shown how this relates to employment and work; that is to economic activity. Here we introduce the distinction in the context of non-economic activity, that is in relation to what we term 'social obligations' (subsuming Parker's categories of work and non-work obligations) and 'leisure'. Our framework is represented diagramatically in Figure 3. We shall illustrate in the discussion which follows the kinds of practices which we categorize as non-economic activities.

As in Chapter 7, in order to allow for flexibility in their categorization we locate various activities on a map of formality/informality, this time, however, in terms of social obligation and leisure. The same rationale lies behind this approach to non-economic activity as lay behind our conceptualization of economic activity, with one added feature. Not only can we connect a particular non-economic practice with one category of non-economic activities under one set of circumstances, while relating it to another under changed circumstances, but, more important in the context of our critique of Hoggett and Bishop, we can allow for the transformation of a non-economic practice into an economic practice under different circumstances, thus allowing it to be connected to other categories of economic activity. In this sense, Figure 3 should be viewed as an extension of Figure 2 (see Chapter 7). We will expand upon the activities included in Figure 3 before concluding this chapter by specifying the implications of this approach for Hoggett and Bishop's analysis.

Jury service is a good example of a *legal obligation*. Not only is there a social obligation to make oneself available for jury service in the United Kingdom but this obligation has the sanction of law. A valid reason for refusing to do jury service is required if this obligation is to be avoided. What is interesting about jury service in the United Kingdom, however, is that financial remuneration over and above legitimate expenses is available, in order to recompense the jurors for earnings lost, if they are in

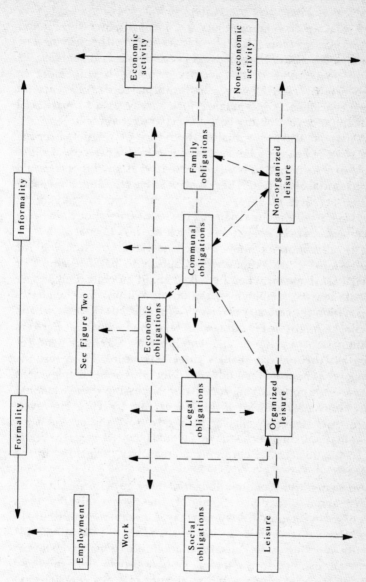

Figure 3 Forms of non-economic activity

employment and the employer withholds payment for the period of absence. There are, therefore, grounds for categorizing jury service as an economic activity (i.e. income generating) under certain circumstances. If a false declaration of either expenses or an employer's intent to stop wages accompanied jury service, we might also designate the activity criminal, having more in keeping with fraud. However, in the normal course of events it is more sensible to conceptualize jury service as a formal social obligation, devoid of any economic characteristics.

We would also conceptualize the return of a national census form by the head of a household as within this category. Failure to return such a form is against the law; as such it is clearly a formal social obligation. There is no possible economic dimension to the activity, however, so it has no scope for categorical movement within our scheme. This is not true of our next two examples of social obligations, which are less formal.

The allocation of time by an individual to studying for professional examinations would appear to be an example of what Parker meant when he talked about an obligation arising out of the work (employment) situation. Within our scheme this falls within the category of *economic obligations*. For example, a bank employee might be encouraged to take the Institute of Bankers examinations by his or her employer as a requirement for progress through the bank's career structure. However, the employee is not paid for study time. Nor is his or her employment dependent upon studying for, sitting or passing these examinations, only advancement within the career structure. However, were paid leave available to study for and/or sit such examinations then such studying would move towards the realm of economic activity, becoming increasingly formalized in the process.

An element of economic obligation may be discerned in many other social situations. Some of these have already been discussed in Chapter 7. A woman may, for example, contribute to the informal, social side of her husband's job: entertaining his clients or acting as his consort on public occasions are instances of being 'married to the job'. For many people, both men and women, a social network and a calendar of social occasions are part of the employment package. Participation may be more or less avoidable – for some it will be compulsory, for others optional – but in most cases it will be the context for seeking preferment and 'playing the game' as a sensible career investment. The distinction between employment/work and leisure may be a difficult one to sustain. How, for example, should one categorize a game of golf with the boss, attendance at a public dinner by a senior local government officer, or a self-employed bricklayer seeing one of his mates down the pub about a job?

Moving across the continuum of social obligation in the direction of informality, we come to *communal obligations*, of which the giving of blood is an interesting example. In the United Kingdom the blood transfusion service is dependent upon the voluntary donation of blood. No financial remuneration is forthcoming for the donation of this valuable resource. The giving of blood in the UK has been described by Richard Titmuss as a 'gift relationship'. The motives of individuals for giving blood vary, but nearly 80 per cent of respondents in the London University study of voluntary blood donors exhibited a high sense of social responsibility towards the needs of other members of the society in accounting for their actions (Titmuss,1970:319). However, were donating blood to become a financially remunerated activity, as it is in the United States, for example, the motives of the blood-donating population might change dramatically. Under these circumstances, the donation of blood might reasonably be expected to be coloured by economic considerations.

Staying with communal social obligations, lift-sharing during the journey to work is another example. This might take the form of co-employees taking it in turn to use their cars to transport the group to work. Where one of their number is unable to reciprocate in kind then a financial contribution towards the cost of petrol may be a substitute. There are good grounds for imagining an economic dimension to this activity: the sharing of car space is clearly undertaken so as to reduce cost and there may also be an element of profit involved. It is not necessarily a purely financial transaction, however. Factors such as neighbourliness and informal community social pressure may also be influential. Car-pooling is an example of a practice which displays greatly varying characteristics, depending on the situation, oscillating between the economic and the non-economic. It is likely, in fact, to exhibit both at once. Neighbouring is another example of the communal social obligation. Here, however, there is less potential for movement into the realm of the economic. With voluntary work and communal self-help, as already discussed in the previous chapter, the distinction between the non-economic and the economic becomes less clear. Much will depend upon the nature of the situation in question.

Finally, and overlapping to a considerable degree with the previous category, there are *family obligations*. Once again, many of the topics which we have discussed in Chapter 7 may appear in some guise within this category: household labour and self-provisioning, in particular. Once again, the distinction between the economic and the non-economic may not always be clear-cut; the private domain of the family may become bound up with the public affairs of organizations and institutions. As an example of these complexities, the recruitment of employees via informal social networks may be illustrative (Jenkins, 1986: 135–50). From the point of view of the employing organizations, 'word of mouth' recruitment serves a number of purposes related to the ease and cost of recruitment, the maintenance of good industrial relations, and the hiring of supposedly 'manageable' workers. From the point of view of the mediator, frequently already an employee of the organization in question, family or other relationships may be strengthened, status within the community enhanced and the obligation to 'look after your own' met. From the point of view of the job-seeker, it is simply easier to get hired. Once he or she is hired, however, the instrumental concerns of the employer interact with the self-interest of the mediator – who will not wish to be 'let down' by the new recruit – to ensure that a complex of familial and communal pressure, expressed as an obligation towards the mediator, is mobilized to ensure his or her acceptable behaviour at the work-place.

Our discussion so far of various kinds of social obligation has illustrated another set of complexities, adding further heterogeneity to our model. The nature of obligation is as context-dependent as the other variables we have examined. A legal obligation is clearly very different indeed from a condition which one is only required to meet in order to gain career advancement. Both of these are qualitatively different from the obligation which is an informally specified aspect of either the performance of a paid job or the social expectations and demands which are enforced by the sanctions of family and community life. Very few – if any – obligations are equally binding upon all people in all circumstances.

We have, however, only scratched the surface of the range of activities which might, under specific circumstances, be described as social obligations. The same is true for the discussion of leisure which follows. In providing illustrations of the activities within the domain of leisure, we will also draw some conclusions concerning the validity of Hoggett and Bishop's analysis.

To look at *organized leisure* first, the voluntary organization of communal leisure group activities – the subject of Hoggett and Bishop's book – is best conceptualized perhaps as formality (of differing degrees) within leisure. The organizing committee of a sports club, for example, is made up of interested individuals who give of their free time in the pursuit of a specific interest. To describe such activity as economic is misguided. To allocate it a market value as a part of the informal economy, is, as we have already argued, wrong (even if estimating the value of every informal economic activity were helpful, which it is not). An individual's participation in such organizations may, what is more, cease to be voluntary; it may become a social obligation created and reproduced by the network of relationships within which the individual is situated. Under such circumstances the activity is best conceptualized as a social obligation, more informal than formal. It is only when it has taken on the characteristics of an informal social obligation that the activity may begin to acquire anything approaching an economic dimension as 'work'. The potential for a leisure activity to become an economic activity, whether formal or informal, will depend on a variety of factors, none of which are intrinsic to the organized activity itself.

Concerned informality in leisure – *non-organised leisure* in the terms of Figure 3 – we draw a distinction between activities which are undertaken individually, which might be described as self-provisioning in leisure, and activities which require co-operation between people in order to be undertaken successfully. The use of the distinction between the organized and the non-organized should be understood in a strictly defined sense. All social activities are, of course, organized to a greater or lesser degree. Not all, however, exist within the context of recognized organizations, whether formal or informal. It is the absence or presence of an organization which is the defining criterion of our distinction. We stay with the sporting theme in our examples but the distinction is just as applicable to other forms of leisure activity.

Jogging is an example of self-provisioning in leisure. It does not require another's presence. It can be undertaken at any time. There are no necessary constraints upon it as an activity, save a minimal physical fitness on the part of the actor, the availability of time and the accessibility of suitable terrain. However we can envisage the categorization of this activity under various headings. Where arrangements are made to jog with others, then the activity might be perceived as operating more in the realm of social obligation. Where joggers form themselves into a club then a degree of formality may be the outcome for those undertaking the organization. The same conditions then come into play as were outlined in the case of the sports club committee.

For individual joggers, membership of a club may place them in a similar, although not identical position, to the members of a football team. In team sports of this kind, an individual may feel a greater social obligation to fellow team members inasmuch as the team may be incomplete in their absence. Competitive team sports would appear to present a particularly mobile category of leisure activity with a strong propensity for movement into informal social obligation, on the one hand, and a degree of formality, on the other. Nor are these necessarily contradictory. Team sports may also, of course, be pursued as economic activities.

The basic point which we are making is that a commonsense classification of a general range of activities as 'leisure' will not suffice for sociological analysis. The same activity may, for example, be undertaken for different reasons. In a certain context it might constitute leisure. In another context it might not. Individual reasons for undertaking an activity cannot be separated from the context within which the activity is undertaken. We believe that our framework, as outlined in Figure 3, allows for more accurate depiction of activities which on the surface appear to be the same, and the relationships between them, than the analyses of the authors we have discussed. It is Hoggett and Bishop's conceptualization of leisure activities as a homogeneous category which lies at the bottom of our critique of their work. This is also the source of Pahl's comment about their attempts to inflate the GDP.

While some leisure group activities may be formally organized by either the private sector or by local government, this does not mean that those buying their leisure opportunities are no longer engaging in leisure pursuits. Alternatively, those who perceive themselves as voluntarily providing, in the course of their own leisure activity, opportunities for others to obtain leisure opportunities at no charge, are not engaging in an economic activity to which a market value can be attached. Those who organize communal leisure group activities without getting paid for it, but without actually volunteering their labour in the sense of being motivated by disinterested enthusiasm or commitment, may be engaging in an activity which has some kind of economic dimension. However, only detailed analysis of the particular situation can decide *which* activities and in *what* ways they partake of the characteristics of economic activity.

In these two sections we have concentrated our attention upon two arguments. First, the distinction between economic and non-economic activity is far from clear-cut. It is a continuum of situationally defined criteria, rather than a sharp differentiation. Second, defining leisure in terms of the absence or presence of constraint or choice is fraught with similar problems. In addition, there are more serious problems concerning how one is to define those notions at all. Once again, there is no firm line to be drawn. Both of these issues are of relevance to the final topic to be discussed in this chapter, the coming of a post-industrial or leisure society.

A leisure society?

One of the more enduring philosophical strands in social science thinking, across a wide range of disciplines is – for want of a better name – 'utopian social evolutionism': the belief that progress is the natural lot of humanity, that society moves upwards from worse to better with the march of science and rationality, and that this ascent is predictable (if not inevitable). Although Weber was refreshingly free from such delusions, both Marx and Durkheim, each in their own way, subscribed to models of social progress of this kind.

A key element in these progressive theories of social change has been the importance of industrialism and technology as the engines of historical development. In many of the most recent variations upon this theme, the greater availability of leisure has played a significant role, being seen as either an indicator of change or its cause. Kerr and his associates, for example, talking about the 'pluralistic industrialism' which they see as an increasingly ubiquitous form of society, argue that,

> The great new freedom may come in the leisure time of individuals. Higher standards of living, more free time and more education make this not only possible but almost inevitable. Leisure will be the happy hunting ground for the independent spirit.
>
> (Kerr *et al.*, 1973:276)

Similar notions can be found in writings about the 'post-industrial society' which forecast that new technology – particularly with respect to knowledge transfer and information processing – will liberate large sections of the population from the grind of boring, unskilled employment. The post-industrial society is 'a society where choice, flexibility, spontaneity and self-determination in mass leisure are maximised' (Rojek, 1985:101). As Kumar has noted (1978), there is a wide variety of models of post-industrial society on offer. These range from the conservative vision of the information society (Bell, 1974) to post-industrial socialism (Gorz, 1982). Across the board, however, there is an assumption that more time will be available for leisure pursuits and less time will, of necessity, be spent in the realm of economic activity.

We do not intend to mount a comprehensive critique of such predictions here. There are, however, a number of points at which our arguments concerning informal economic activity articulate with debates about the post-industrial or leisure society. As we have already discussed in Chapter 3, the informal economy models developed by authors such as Gershuny and Handy have some of their roots in arguments about the nature of post-industrial society which were current in the 1970s. More to the point, however, in the context of this chapter, are the implications of our discussion about the nature of leisure, obligation and economic activity for theories of post-industrialism and the leisure society.

Reviewing the arguments of authors such as Bell, Gorz, Kerr and Kumar, there are several key issues which are relevant here. First, despite the sensitivity displayed by some of these authors with respect to the heterogeneous and complex nature of economic activity, there is a common tendency to adopt a relatively simple definition of leisure. To put the matter even more accurately, leisure is generally not defined at all. It is either treated commonsensically – as if 'everybody knows' what leisure is – or it is conceptualized as a residual category, simply the absence of employment or work. As we have already argued, the distinction between the economic and the non-economic is not, in general, hard and fast. It is, rather, context specific. Many practices partake of both economic and non-economic dimensions, sometimes simultaneously. Defining leisure, and thinking about the relationships between leisure, social obligation, work and employment, requires subtlety and care. The existence of leisure merely in the absence of work or employment should not be inferred or taken for granted.

This point is of some importance for the argument. Post-industrial society is typically conceptualized as involving not only *less* work or employment, but also *more* leisure. Such an argument would seem to require, for the sake of intellectual coherence and credibility, a better definition of leisure than that currently on offer. Despite our earlier harsh comments about Gershuny and Handy, their work is, at least in part, an attempt to remedy this shortcoming.

Second, and it is a criticism which is closely related to the remarks immediately above, one of the few positive features of the notions of leisure used by the authors in question is an emphasis upon choice. This, as we have already suggested in earlier sections, is a difficult concept, to say the least. Difficult to define and difficult to demonstrate. Nor is it value-free. All the more reason, therefore, for exercising great caution in its use. This is also an important point for the general argument, inasmuch as post-industrial society is perceived as offering the hope of a degree of liberation from the mundane drudgery of industrial tasks and greater scope for the individual exercise of choice. Enhanced freedom is also held out by Kerr *et al.* as an (almost) inevitable consequence of the development of industrial society. Their 'pluralistic industrialism' partakes, in fact, of many of the characteristics of post-industrial society. If our arguments are correct, however, the potential for greater freedom in such a situation must, at best, be taken as not proven.

Which brings us to the third and final point. Philosophical and other problems concerning the nature of choice and freedom aside, notions of the post-industrial leisure society collide awkwardly with the realities of life in the social-democratic market economies of the western world in the 1980s. Such, of course, is the unfortunate lot of the futurologist; in Giddens' words, writing about Gorz, visions of post-industrial society are at risk from 'the perils of punditry' (1987:274). The post-industrial society which we are presently experiencing – if such indeed it may be called – is a very different place than that imagined, for example, by an author such as Daniel Bell. There is, undoubtedly, more time available to the population for leisure. There is also little doubt that, as a consequence of a revolution in telecommunications and information technology, on the one hand, and the expansion of commercial leisure services, on the other, there are more and more varied opportunities for leisure available. However, for many of the people about whom we are talking, their greater 'leisure time' is *enforced* leisure time. One person's leisure is someone else's idle time. For unemployed people in particular, the absence of employment does not mean the availability of leisure. If for no other reason, this is because the greater leisure opportunities presently on offer generally require economic resources if they are to be taken, resources which the unemployed are not usually able to mobilize (and certainly not for leisure pursuits). This is where the distinction between the economic and the non-economic begins to break down again. What, for one person, is a pleasurable leisure activity may be part of a low-paid and unsatisfying job for someone else. For a third person it may be a profitable component of their investment portfolio. For a fourth, it may be a luxury which financial circumstances prevent them from allowing their children to participate in. Even non-commercial leisure activities are not, as a rule, costless, whether in terms of social or economic resources.

   In such a context, therefore, notions of choice and freedom, if not absurdities, are certainly luxuries. Access to leisure is not uniformly distributed across the population. This is particularly the case for those leisure opportunities which are regulated by market relationships, but it applies also to other forms of leisure. As with informal economic activity, a whole host of factors, of which access to and control over resources may be the most influential, determine *who* partakes of *which* leisure activities.

This is what Touraine means when he talks about the 'social stratification of leisure activities' in post-industrial society (1974:207). And, of course, this is the central weakness of many discussions of post-industrial society. In stressing 'industrialism' as the defining feature of western social democracies – usually at the expense of any discussion of capitalism – structuring relations of domination, exploitation and exclusion are glossed over (Clarke and Critcher, 1985:196–8; Rojek, 1985:103). The post-industrial societies of Europe and North America are, before they are anything else, capitalist societies.

To summarize, we have argued that models of the post-industrial leisure society founder for a number of reasons. In the first place, they have simply been overtaken by events. The post-industrial society, such as it is, which characterizes many of the abandoned industrial heartlands of capitalist development fulfils few of the optimists' predictions. Second, the notions of industrial society which provide these analyses with much of their theoretical content are inadequate for the analytical task in hand. Finally, the centrality of leisure to models of post-industrial society is a particular problem, inasmuch as the distinction between the economic and the non-economic is less clear cut than many of the authors concerned assume. The equation of leisure with freedom and choice is similarly misguided.

With respect to these final comments, there is an obvious similarity between our critique of models of the 'informal economy' and our comments about forecasts of a 'leisure society'. Both empirically and theoretically, neither stands up intact to the rigours of close and sceptical examination. Neither offers a diagnosis or a resolution of the pressing social and economic problems which they address. There is, in fact, no informal economy or leisure society as such. There is, rather, an ever-widening gulf between those who have the resources to engage in informal economic activity or indulge their tastes for leisure and those who do not. If there is a post-industrial society in the making, it is in that gulf that many of its defining features are to be found.

Chapter 9

THE MYTH OF THE HIDDEN ECONOMY

In this book we have examined critically a set of notions concerning a particular aspect of the organization and functioning of the market economies of the social democracies of the 'developed' western world which is known as the 'hidden', 'black' or 'informal economy'. Originally formulated as a distinct model by social scientists – typically sociologists, social anthropologists and economists – these ideas have passed into popular usage and the discourse of politicians and policy makers as an influential body of rhetoric. Inasmuch as they are rhetoric, short on conceptual integrity or empirical support, we have called these notions 'the myth of the hidden economy'. As with all myths, this particular creature of the imagination is constructed out of a number of themes. Very briefly, these may be summarized as follows.

First, there is a belief that things are not quite as they seem. Behind the visible facade of daily life there is 'what's really going on'. Taking many forms, from full-blown conspiracy theory to the less sinister view of 'wheels within wheels', this in our context finds its shape as a quest for the 'hidden', 'underground' or 'black economy', a separate economic milieu, somehow distinct from the public domain of commerce, production and finance, with its own characteristic rules and organization.

Second, the separate economy is characterized as a flourishing hive of activity: 'Everybody's at it, aren't they?' This also takes a number of forms. It may be a justification for participation in informal economic activity by an unemployed worker or a self-employed person. A politician may claim that the economy is more healthy than the national accounts reveal it to be, or that only half of those officially registered as unemployed are *really* unemployed. An academic may argue something similar in order to emphasize the urgency of a particular research grant application. And all of these may believe what they say. This is not necessarily a case of cynical deception or the careful management of half-truths.

Finally, there is a considerable degree of ambivalence in social attitudes to the ants toiling in the darkness, hidden away under the stone of public life. For some commentators, there is a problem. The *demi-monde* of the hidden economy is for them inhabited by parasites, living off the state but busy at the same time making money. There is a large range of folk-devils inhabiting this particular underworld: 'racketeers', 'crooks', 'spivs', 'drones', 'scroungers', 'lay-abouts', 'cowboys' and 'shady operators', to mention but a few. From another moral and political viewpoint, there are protests about 'exploitation', 'scab labour', 'union busting' and 'sweatshops'. Health and safety at work is also an issue. And there is, of course, always the problem of tax evasion (although this never seems to loom as large in the rhetoric of politicians as welfare scrounging). All in all, there are several perspectives from which the hidden economy is seen as a problem. Taxes must be collected, social security abuses stamped out, working conditions controlled and the economy in general regulated.

The hidden economy may, however, be viewed in another light, as the last refuge of untrammelled enterprise in an over-rigid economic system. For economic growth to be achieved and sustained, enterprise must be encouraged, not stifled. Better to work in low-paid, poorly protected jobs than to be dependent upon state welfare provision. This is good for informal workers, whose self-reliance and independence are maintained, good for the rest of the population, who pay less for certain goods and services, and good for the state, inasmuch as public expenditure can be curtailed and the money supply controlled. The existence of an alternative economy serves to put downward pressure on wages in the 'visible' economy, further fostering enterprise, promoting growth and curbing inflation. According to this view, what is needed is less, not more, regulation. This model of the situation should be familiar to most readers and does not require further elaboration.

There is also another positive view of the hidden economy. This rests upon the straightforward and secure foundation of self-interest rather than the flimsy scaffolding of abstract economics. Even though it may be a bad thing for *other* people to earn a 'bit on the side', there is little to suggest that for most people such an attitude of disapproval extends to their own behaviour: after all, everybody else does it. The language which is used to describe informal economic activity betrays the ambivalence with which it is evaluated. A host of expressions are used to distance informal economic activity from other forms of work or employment: 'hobbles', 'foreigners', 'doing the double', 'moonlighting', 'a bit on the side', 'homers' and many others. Gerald Mars notes the distinction between the 'perk' and the 'fiddle'. *My* perks are *your* fiddles. We use language thus to mask and manage a contradiction: what we do ourselves (or would do, given the opportunity) we may condemn in others. The ambivalence which we are describing here is probably most keenly felt by those on the right of the political spectrum. It is the conflict between economic liberalism and political authoritarianism. On the left, there may be a tension between support for economic and industrial regulation, on the one hand, and anti-authoritarianism, on the other. There are probably few people who do not, at some level, have mixed feelings about informal economic activity.

The myth of the hidden economy, therefore, has three distinct aspects. First, there is the separate economy (or economies) model. The belief that this economy is booming is the second. Third, evaluations of the hidden economy are frequently ambivalent and contradictory. In examining the way in which this understanding of the economic systems of western social democratic states has developed, we have come to reject its utility, either for analytical purposes or the more urgent ends of policy formulation and implementation. We have a number of reasons for our conclusions, which we shall now discuss in turn.

To look first at the distinction between the *formal* and the *informal*, we do not believe that it is possible to draw a firm, sharp line between them, as separate domains of social experience. There is, to be sure, a distinction to be made, but it is a distinction between the ends of a continuum. The criteria which differentiate the one from the other are by no means clear. Is it simply a general contrast between the written and the oral, is it a more definite set of criteria, related to the presence or absence of bureaucratic regulation, or is it more specific again, the presence or absence of state regulation? Rather than a single criterion or set of criteria, we suggest that there are degrees of formality and informality, depending on the context. Most social interaction partakes of a degree of each. As we have argued in earlier chapters, social life in modern industrial societies occurs within a complicated framework of legal and administrative regulation. However, as we have also argued, even the most formal contexts are comprehensively penetrated by and implicated in informal social relationships.

The key to understanding the relationship between informality and formality lies in adopting an historical perspective. As we have argued in several places above, there are two long-term processes, interconnected but analytically distinct, which underlie any distinction which we might wish to draw between formality and informality. The first is the development of writing and information technology, the second the rise of bureaucratic rationality and the modern state. The first is a necessary condition of the second. Each has been important in the gradual definition and expansion of formal social relations and institutions. However, and this is of considerable importance, while it is true that without formality there can be no informality, the informal is much more than a residual category. Formality and informality – as models for the conduct of social interaction – exist in the context of each other's presence. Each has particular qualities and characteristics, defined within an oppositional relationship to the other, but each has also, through a process of historical development, come to signify a distinct and peculiar way of doing things: 'going by the book' as opposed to 'give and take'. To reiterate our earlier argument, the informal is both an absence and a presence within the formal, and vice versa. The relationship between them is a contradictory dialectic of dependence and autonomy.

Next, there is the distinction between the *economic* and the *non-economic* to consider. Once again, it seems more appropriate to conceptualize these as opposite ends of a continuum rather than sharply differentiated categories. If for no other reason, this is because the bulk of the research material to which we have referred in the course of preceding chapters permits of no other interpretation. Economic activity is socially organized; social interaction proceeds within a framework of resource distribution and consumption. In one sense, it is as simple as that.

There is, however, also a more profound point to be made. The categories of the 'economic' and the 'non-economic' are neither objective nor natural. As with all conceptual devices, they are culturally and historically specific. This is so in two respects. First, the basic distinction itself, the dichotomization of social experience into distinct domains of the economic and the non-economic, is not to be taken for granted. Not all societies divide human experience in this way. Second, even in those cultural contexts which are structured by such a dichotomization, the allocation of specific activities to one or the other category varies across time and situation. Nor is the distinction uniformly significant for all actors.

This is simply to reiterate the substantivist argument in economic anthropology: the presence and nature of classificatory categories which we can translate in analytical terms as the 'economic' and the 'non-economic' is a matter for investigation rather than thoughtless presumption or over-rigid theorization. In the kind of societies on which we focus in this book, the existence – and, indeed, the importance – of such categories, as central structuring principles of interaction, is not to be doubted. The specific nature and content of these notions, however, remains to be documented in each situation. We will discuss this issue further below. While the distinction between the poles of the economic/non-economic continuum may be reasonably straightforward, there is a large middle ground where matters are less clear-cut.

To say this is to put actors' conceptions and categorizations of their own activities at the centre of our definitional exercise. A stress upon folk models of the economic and the non-economic (and the nature of each) is not, of course, to deny the social scientist a role in the formulation of analytical categories. However, such an emphasis does – or, rather, should – make it more difficult to fall into either of two errors which we have identified in the course of our discussion. The first, most clearly exemplified, perhaps, in the work of Henry, is the argument that particular activities are not really economic, despite the insistence of the actors concerned to the contrary. The second is the attempt to attach a financial or otherwise economic value to too broad a range of activities. Hoggett and Bishop's discussion of leisure is a good example of this, as are many of the attempts to measure the value of the informal economy. Both of these errors, each in their own way, stem from the drawing of an over-simple boundary between the economic and non-economic, on the one hand, and the use of a notion of the economic which is conceived in absolute or 'objective' terms, on the other.

The issue of *measurement* is also central to our critique of the 'myth of the hidden economy'. In Chapter 5, in particular, we have documented various attempts to quantify and place a value upon informal economic activity. We are not the first to conclude that many of these attempts, if not absurd, are misguided. Leaving aside specific criticisms of particular approaches and methods, particularly with respect to the indirect indicators of informal economic activity which they employ, there are a number of general points which can be made in this context. First, it seems to us that many measures of the informal economy are dictated more by political or policy-related expediency than anything else. As a consequence, normal standards of rigour may be relaxed in a process not of hypothesis testing but of hypothesis verification. Second, the process of measurement depends, of necessity, upon the allocation of objects or phenomena to discrete categories, differentiated from other categories by boundary criteria. In so doing, over-sharp distinctions, of a kind which we have rejected above, are fostered. The situation is made worse when one considers that, because of the unreliability, poverty or otherwise problematic nature of the aggregate data which is the basis of most measurement exercises, the categories of differentiation employed are typically nominal (either/or) rather than ordinal (graded along a con-tinuum). Finally, and related to these points, although informal economic activity may, like any other kind of activity, be measurable in terms of its frequency, the attribution of financial value to certain kinds of informal economic activity, which is the basis of the valuations of the informal economy offered by many writers, is, to say the least, problematic. It is symptomatic of a vulgar materialism which, to adopt a memorable phrase originally coined by Veblen, seeks to impose the canons of 'pecuniary culture' upon the fabric of all aspects of social life.

Which brings us back, of course, to the distinction between the economic and the non-economic. Attempts to estimate the value of informal economic activity, in terms of national accounts or whatever, throw into sharp relief the problems which beset the discussion in this respect. We have argued in earlier chapters that value, as defined within conventional economics, requires the existence of a market. Financial value, by extension, requires the existence of a cash market. For the products of many kinds of informal economic activity, whether goods or services, there is no certainty that an appropriate market, whether cash or otherwise, actually exists. In some circumstances where a market may function, it may not do so in all places or at all times.

Is it, in fact, possible to describe a particular activity as economic in the absence of a market context, of whatever kind? This question is critically dependent upon whether one adopts *production* or *exchange* as the essence of economic activity. A marxist economist is likely to choose the former, a liberal economist, the latter. A stress upon production allows for the possibility of economic activity which does not necessarily exist within a market framework. We have been implicitly arguing for a definition of this kind. Hence the stress upon work. However, bearing in mind our other argument, that actors' categorizations of their own activity should be the basis for the formulation of analytical models, we must acknowledge that there is a large area of considerable uncertainty, most particularly where the categories of *work* and *social obligation* overlap. This is why, as in our Figures 2 and 3, we not only conceive of economic and non-economic activity as lying along a continuum, but also visualize more specific categories of economic activity as mobile in terms of their location within our analytical framework.

To sum up the discussion so far, we offer three basic criticisms of the 'myth of the hidden economy'. First, the distinction between informality and formality is not clear-cut or unambiguous. The two alternatives represent the poles of a continuum, between which exists a spectrum of graduated differentiae. Much the same can be said, second, about the distinction between economic and non-economic activities. Third, and related to these criticisms, we suggest that most attempts to establish the value of the hidden economy have been misguided and unreliable.

Our argument may be encapsulated by saying that we do not believe there is any such thing as *the* hidden economy, *the* informal economy, *the* black economy, or whatever. Notions of this sort lack empirical support. Nor are they characterized by either theoretical elegance or argumentative rigour. There are no separate economies as such, only the well-darned and seamed web that is the complexity (and confusion) of a social-democratic market economy. Most informal economic activity is not particularly hidden, although it may be invisible for certain limited administrative purposes. Similarly, informality and formality are chronically implicated in each other in the routine business of social life. Rarely, if ever, do we encounter either in a pristine, unsullied state.

To say this, however, is not to deny the usefulness of talking about (more or less) informal economic activity. The analytical framework which we have developed permits the topic to be taken seriously without the reification or simplification of social reality towards which much of the research reviewed in earlier chapters tends. In theoretical terms, our model is constructed in the intersection of two long-term historical processes in western society. The first of these is the development of capitalist social and economic relations, entailing the gradual elaboration of a distinction between the economic and the non-economic and, more specifically, between work and employment. Second, there is the spread of literacy and the rise of bureaucracy and the modern state, which has engendered and incrementally rendered more significant the contrast between formal and informal relations. Within this general theoretical framework, the interrelationship of particular categories of economic and non-economic activity may be investigated.

By situating our analysis within an understanding of capitalist development and the evolution of bureaucracy and the modern state, we explicitly place issues of *power*, *authority* and *control* at the centre of the account. One of the most consistent threads to emerge during our discussion of the literature is that informal economic activity, much as other economic activity, is hierarchically structured in terms of access, rewards and experience. There are three particularly important structuring principles which contribute to the hierarchical organization of informal economic activity.

First, there is formal employment status: whether an individual is, for bureaucratic purposes, self-employed, employed or unemployed. Participation in informal activity is dependent to a large degree upon access to both social and economic resources. There is a considerable amount of research which demonstrates that unemployment, particularly long-term unemployment, substantially curtails access to both. Most obviously, the economic resources of individuals and families decline. Less obvious, but no less important, is the decline in social resources: contacts, information, reputation, etc. The consequence of this situation – moral panics about 'welfare scroungers' notwithstanding – is that the unemployed are the least likely people to engage in informal economic activity.

Second, more generally, class is also an influential factor. Clearly, the likelihood of experiencing unemployment is a function of class. There are, however, other things bound up in class identity: type of housing, residential location, kind of employment or work, health and education, to list only the more obvious. These determine the nature of the social and economic resources which can be brought to bear on the pursuit of informal economic opportunities. Here, however, it is not simply a question of access to such opportunities. Class also affects both the kind of informal economic activity which is carried on by people in particular contexts and the penalties which attach to those activities which are legally or customarily proscribed.

Third, as we have illustrated in several places, gender is of tremendous importance in deciding the nature of informal economic activity. 'Women's work' is both formal and informal. In both cases the experience of, and rewards which derive from, economic activity are structured by a gendered division of labour. The issue of gender is also of particular significance for our theoretical position because, as we argued in Chapter 7, women's domestic labour is one of the clearest examples of the interdependence and interpenetration of formal and informal economic activity.

There are other factors which structure access to, and the experience of, informal economic activity. Age, ethnicity and geography – in particular, the urban-rural continuum – are obviously important. From the evidence which we have reviewed, however, formal employment status, class and gender should be considered the most significant. Just as with formal economic activity, informal economic activity is characterized by inequality, stratification and heterogeneous social experience. They are part of the same economic system, concerned with resource production, allocation and distribution, and are structured by the same principles.

To close our discussion, there is, perhaps, a short digression to be made into the sociology of knowledge. We have argued throughout the preceding chapters that the notion of the informal economy – 'the myth of the hidden economy' as we have called it – is theoretically inadequate, often methodologically weak (if not completely suspect) and empirically unsubstantiated. In short, in so far as it is ever possible to offer such a judgement, it is *wrong*. Even some of its keenest proponents, such as Pahl, for example, have come round eventually to such a conclusion. If it *is* wrong, however, the questions have to be asked, why was it so enthusiastically proposed and publicized in the first place, and, even more interesting, why in the face of a fairly consistent body of criticism and undermining evidence, has it survived so long as an important area of research and discourse?

To answer these questions adequately would, of course, require another book. However, a preliminary answer might point to the intersection of *intellectual* developments in the social sciences, *institutional* concerns with research fund-raising in an era of contraction in higher education, and, most critical of all perhaps, *political* concerns with the presentation and legitimation of policy options in the context of historically high and unacceptable levels of unemployment. Of the three, it seems likely that intellectual concerns were the least important in the promotion of the myth, although they may have been vital to its genesis. It is difficult to resist the conclusion that the progress of research and theorization in this area has been largely determined by institutional and political concerns. It is, however, a telling reflection on the political environment within which academic research currently takes place, and the professional climate within the research community, that, criticisms and evidence notwithstanding, the survival of the 'myth of the hidden economy' seems assured for the foreseeable future.

BIBLIOGRAPHY

Aldrich, H., Jones, T.P. and McEvoy, D. (1984), 'Ethnic advantage and minority business development', in R. Ward and R. Jenkins (eds), *Ethnic Communities in Business: Strategies for Economic Survival*, Cambridge, Cambridge University Press.

Allen, S. and Wolkowitz, C. (1986), 'The control of women's labour: the case of homeworking', *Feminist Review*, no. 22: 25–51.

Allen, S. and Wolkowitz, C. (1987), *Homeworking: Myths and Realities*, London, Macmillan.

Arensberg, C.M. (1939), *The Irish Countryman: An Anthropological Study*, New York, Macmillan.

Arensberg, C.M. and Kimball, S.T. (1940), *Family and Community in Ireland*, London, Peter Smith.

Arlacchi, P. (1986), *Mafia Business: The Mafia Ethic and the Spirit of Capitalism*, London, Verso.

Aschenbrenner, J. (1975), *Lifelines: Black Families in Chicago*, New York, Holt, Rinehart and Winston.

Barnes, J.A. (1980), *Who Should Know What? Social Science, Privacy and Ethics*, revised edition, Cambridge, Cambridge University Press.

Barrett, S.R. (1984), 'Racism, ethics and the subversive nature of anthropological inquiry', *Philosophy of the Social Sciences*, vol. 14: 1–25.

Becker, H.S. (1963), *Outsiders: Studies in the Sociology of Deviance*, New York, Free Press.

Bell, C. and Newby, H. (1971), *Community Studies*, London, Allen and Unwin.

Bell, D. (1974), *The Coming of the Post-Industrial Society*, London, Heinemann.

Bennett, T. and Wright, R. (1984), *Burglars on Burglary: Prevention and the Offender*, Aldershot, Gower.

Bequai, A. (1978a), *Computer Crime*, Lexington, Mass, D.C. Heath.

Bequai, A. (1978b), *White Collar Crime: A 20th Century Crisis*, Lexington, Mass, D.C. Heath.

Berger, P. (1975), 'The human shape of work', in G. Esland, G. Salaman and M. Speakman (eds), *People and Work*, London, Holmes and McDougall.

Bhachu, P. (1985), *Twice Migrants: East African Sikh Settlers in Britain*, London, Tavistock.

Blau, P.M. and Scott, W.R. (1963), *Formal Organizations: A Comparative Approach*, London, Routledge and Kegan Paul.

Blok, A. (1974), *The Mafia of a Sicilian Village 1860–1960*, Oxford, Basil Blackwell.

Boissevain, J. (1984), 'Small entrepreneurs in contemporary Europe', in R. Ward and R. Jenkins (eds), *Ethnic Communities in Business: Strategies for Economic Survival*, Cambridge, Cambridge University Press.

Bott, E. (1971), *Family and Social Network*, second edition, London, Tavistock.

Bouquet, M. (1984), 'Women's work in rural south-west England', in N. Long (ed.), *Family and Work in Rural Societies: Perspectives on Non-Wage Labour*, London, Tavistock.

Box, S. (1981), *Deviance, Reality and Society*, second edition, London, Holt, Rinehart and Winston.

Boyle, G.E. (1984), 'In search of Ireland's black economy', *Irish Banking Review*, March, 32–42.

Brightbill, C.K. (1963), *The Challenge of Leisure*, Englewood Cliffs, NJ, Prentice-Hall.

Bromley, R. and Gerry, C. (eds) (1979), *Casual Work and Poverty in Third World Cities*, Chichester, John Wiley.

Brown, M. (1974), *Sweated Labour: A Study of Homework*, Low Pay Pamphlet No. 3, London, Low Pay Unit.

Brown, R. (1978), 'Work', in P. Abrams (ed.), *Work, Urbanism and Inequality: UK Society Today*, London, Weidenfeld and Nicolson.

Brown, R. (1985) 'Attitudes to Work, Occupational identity and industrial change', in B. Roberts, R. Finnegan and D. Gallie (eds), *New Approaches to Economic Life, Economic Restructuring: Unemployment and the Social Division of Labour*, Manchester, Manchester University Press.

Bryant, J. (1982), 'An introductory bibliography to work on the informal economy in third world literature', in J. Laite (ed.), *Bibliographies on Labour Markets and the Informal Economy*, London, SSRC.

Bulmer, M. (ed.) (1982), *Social Research Ethics*, London, Macmillan.

Bulmer, M. (1986), *Neighbours: The Work of Philip Abrams*, Cambridge, Cambridge University Press.

Bulmer, M. (1987), *The Social Basis of Community Care*, London, George Allen and Unwin.

Burawoy, M. (1979), *Manufacturing Consent: Changes in the Labor Process under Monopoly Capitalism*, Chicago, University of Chicago Press.

Burns, S. (1977), *The Household Economy*, Boston, Beacon Press.

Burns, T. and Stalker, G.M. (1961), *The Management of Innovation*, London, Tavistock.

Button, K.J. (1984), 'Regional variations in the irregular economy: a study of possible trends', *Regional Studies*, vol. 18: 385–92.

Cassel, D. (1983), 'The growing shadow economy: implications for stabilization policy', presented to the conference on *The Economics of the Shadow Economy*, ZIF, Bielefeld, W. Germany, October.

Chamber of Commerce of the United States (1974), *White Collar Crime*, Chamber of Commerce of the United States, Washington, DC.

Chiplin, B. and Sloane, P.J. (1982), *Tackling Discrimination at the Workplace: An Analysis of Sex Discrimination in Britain*, Cambridge, Cambridge University Press.

Clark, D.Y. (1987), 'Families facing redundancy', in S. Fineman (ed.), *Unemployment: Personal and Social Consequences*, London, Tavistock.

Clarke, J. and Critcher, C. (1985), *The Devil Makes Work: Leisure in Capitalist Britain*, London, Macmillan.

Clegg, S. and Dunkerley, D. (1980), *Organization, Class and Control*, London, Routledge and Kegan Paul.

Connolly, P. (1985), 'The politics of the informal sector: a critique', in N. Redclift and E. Mingione (eds), *Beyond Employment: Household, Gender and Subsistence*, Oxford, Basil Blackwell.

Cormack, R.J., Osborne, R.D. and Thompson, W.T. (1980), 'Into work? Young school leavers and the structure of opportunity in Belfast', *Research Paper 5*, Belfast, Fair Employment Agency.

Cornuel, D. and Duriez, B. (1985), 'Local exchanges and state intervention', in N. Redclift and E. Mingione (eds), *Beyond Employment: Household, Gender and Employment*, Oxford, Basil Blackwell.

Coyle, A. (1984), *Redundant Women*, London, Women's Press.

Cragg, A. and Dawson, T. (1981), 'Qualitative research among homeworkers', *Research Paper No. 21*, London, Department of Employment.

Crine, S. (1979), *The Hidden Army*, London, Low Pay Unit.

Curran, M.M. (1985), *Stereotypes and Selection: Gender and Family in the Recruitment Process*, London, HMSO.

Daniel, W.M. (1963), 'A consideration of individual and group attitudes in expanding and technically changing organizations', unpublished MSc (Tech) thesis, Manchester University.

Davis, J. (1972), 'Gifts and the UK economy', *Man* (n.s.), vol. 7: 408–29.

Davis, J. (1985), 'Rules not laws: outline of an ethnographic approach to economics', in B. Roberts, R. Finnegan and D. Gallie (eds), *New Approaches to Economic Life: Economic Restructuring: Unemployment and the Social Division of Labour*, Manchester, Manchester University Press.

Dearlove, J. and Saunders, P. (1984), *Introduction to British Politics*, Cambridge, Polity.

del Boca, D. and Forte, F. (1982), 'Recent empirical surveys and theoretical interpretations of the parallel economy in Italy', in V. Tanzi (ed.), *The Underground Economy in the United States and Abroad*, Lexington, Mass, D.C. Heath.

Denison, E. (1982), 'Is US growth understated because of the underground economy? Employment ratios suggest not', *Review of Income and Wealth*, series 28, March: 1–16.

Dex, S. (1985), *The Sexual Division of Work*, Brighton, Wheatsheaf.

Dilnot, A. and Morris, C.N. (1981), 'What do we know about the black economy?', *Fiscal Studies*, vol. 2: 58–73.

Ditton, J. (1977), *Part-Time Crime: An Ethnography of Fiddling and Pilferage*,

London, Macmillan.

Doeringer, P.B. and Piore, M.J. (1971), *Internal Labor Markets and Manpower Analysis*, Lexington, Mass, D.C. Heath.

Doig, A. (1984), *Corruption and Misconduct in Contemporary British Politics*, Harmondsworth, Penguin.

Douglas, M. (1973), *Natural Symbols: Exporations in Cosmology*, Harmondsworth, Pelican.

Dumazadier, J. (1960), 'Current problems of the sociology of leisure', *International Social Science Journal*, vol. 12: 552-31.

Driver, C. (1984), 'Testing the Gershuny hypothesis', *Futures*, vol. 16: 508-12.

Edgell, S. and Hart, G. (1988), *Informal Work: A Case Study of Moonlighting Firemen*, Salford Papers in Sociology and Anthropology, Department of Sociology and Anthropology, University of Salford.

Edwards, R.C., Reich, M. and Gordon, D.M. (eds) (1975), *Labor Market Segmentation*, Lexington, Mass, Lexington Books.

Employment Gazette (1983), 'The unemployed: survey estimates for 1981 compared with the monthly count', *Employment Gazette*, vol. 91, no. 6: 265-7.

Employment Gazette (1986), 'Classification of economic activity', *Employment Gazette*, vol. 94, no. 1: 21-7.

Errington, A. (ed.) (1986), *The Farm as a Family Business: An Annotated Bibliography*, Reading, Agricultural Manpower Society.

Fagin, F. (1979), 'Views from three other disciplines: (ii) Psychiatry', in S. Wallman (ed.), *Social Anthropology of Work*, London, Academic Press.

Febvre, L. and Martin, H.-J. (1976), *The Coming of the Book: the Impact of Printing 1450-1800*, London, New Left Books.

Feige, E. (1981), 'The UK's unobserved economy: a preliminary assessment', *Economic Affairs*, vol. 1: 205-12.

Ferman, L.A. and Berndt, L.E. (1981), 'The irregular economy', in S. Henry (ed.), *Can I Have It In Cash? A Study of Informal Institutions and Unorthodox Ways of Doing Things*, London, Astragal Books.

Ferman, L.A., Berndt, L.E. and Selo, E. (1978), 'Analysis of the irregular economy: cash flow in the informal sector', unpublished report of the Bureau of Employment and Training, Michigan Department of Labor and Industrial Relations. The University of Michigan–Wayne State University, Ann Arbor, Michigan.

Ferman, L.A., Henry, S. and Hoyman, M. (eds) (1987), 'The informal economy', *The Annals of the American Academy of Political and Social Science*, vol. 493, *passim*.

Fernandez, J.P. (1982), *Racism and Sexism in Corporate Life*, Lexington, Mass, Lexington Books.

Fevre, R. (1983), 'Employment and unemployment in Port Talbot – a reference paper', working paper, University College, Swansea.

Finch, J. (1983), *Married to the Job: Wives' Incorporation into Men's Work*, London, Allen and Unwin.

Finch, J. and Groves, D. (eds) (1983), *A Labour of Love: Women, Work and Caring*, London, Routledge and Kegan Paul.

Firth, R. (ed.) (1967), *Themes in Economic Anthropology*, London, Tavistock.

Fishburne, P.M. (1980), 'Survey techniques for studying threatening topics: a case study on the use of heroin', unpublished Ph.D. thesis, New York University.

Frankenberg, R. (1957), *Village on the Border*, London, Cohen and West.

Frankenberg, R. (1966), *Communities in Britain: Social Life in Town and Country*, Harmondsworth, Penguin.

Freeman, C. (1982), 'The "understanding employer"', in J. West (ed.), *Work, Women and the Labour Market*, London, Routledge and Kegan Paul.

Freud, D. (1979), 'A guide to underground economics', *Financial Times*, 9 April: 16.

Frey, B.S. and Weck, H. (1981), *Estimating the Shadow Economy: A Naive Approach*, Institute for Empirical and Economic Research, University of Zurich.

Gaertner, W. and Wenig, A. (eds) (1985), *The Economics of the Shadow Economy*, Proceedings of the International Conference on the Economics of the Shadow Economy, University of Bielefeld, West Germany, 10–14 October 1983, Berlin, Springer Verlag.

Garraty, J.A. (1978), *Unemployment in History: Economic Thought and Public Policy*, New York, Harper and Row.

Gavron, H. (1966), *The Captive Wife: Conflicts of Housebound Mothers*, London, Routledge and Kegan Paul.

George, M.D. (1966), *London Life in the Eighteenth Century*, London, Peregrine.

Gershuny, J.I. (1977), 'Post-industrial society: the myth of the service sector', *Futures*, vol. 9: 103–14.

Gershuny, J.I. (1978), *After Industrial Society: the Emerging Self-Service Economy*, London, Macmillan.

Gershuny, J.I. (1983), *Social Innovation and the Division of Labour*, Oxford, Oxford University Press.

Gershuny, J.I. (1985), 'Economic development and change in the mode of provision of services', in N. Redclift and E. Mingione (eds), *Beyond Employment: Household, Gender and Subsistence*, Oxford, Basil Blackwell.

Gershuny, J.I. and Miles, I.D. (1983), *The New Service Economy: the Transformation of Employment in Industrial Society*, London, Frances Pinter.

Gershuny, J.I. and Miles, I.D. (1985), 'Towards a new social economics', in B. Roberts, R. Finnegan and D. Gallie (eds), *New Approaches to Economic Life: Economic Restructuring: Unemployment and the Social Division of Labour*, Manchester, Manchester University Press.

Gershuny, J.I. and Pahl. R.E. (1979), 'Work outside employment: some preliminary speculation', *New Universities Quarterly*, vol. 34: 120–35.

Gershuny, J.I. and Pahl, R.E. (1980), 'Britain in the decade of the three economies', *New Society*, 3 January, vol. 51, no. 900: 7–9.

Gerth, H.H. and Mills, C.W. (1948), *From Max Weber: Essays in Sociology*, London, Routledge and Kegan Paul.

Giddens, A. (1987), *Social Theory and Modern Sociology*, Cambridge, Polity.

Gill, O. (1977), *Luke Street: Housing Policy, Conflict and the Creation of the*

Delinquent Area, London, Macmillan.

Golding, P. and Middleton, S. (1978), 'Why is the press so obsessed with welfare scroungers?', *New Society*, 26 October 1978, vol. 46, no. 838: 195–7.

Golding, P. and Middleton, S. (1982), *Images of Welfare*, Oxford, Martin Robertson.

Goldthorpe, J. (1985), 'The end of convergence: corporatist and dualist tendencies in modern western societies', in B. Roberts, R. Finnegan and D. Gallie (eds), *New Approaches to Economic Life: Economic Restructuring: Unemployment and the Social Division of Labour*, Manchester, Manchester University Press.

Goody, J. (1977), *The Domestication of the Savage Mind*, Cambridge, Cambridge University Press.

Goody, J. (1986), *The Logic of Writing and the Organization of Society*, Cambridge, Cambridge University Press.

Goody, J. (1987), *The Interface Between the Written and the Oral*, Cambridge, Cambridge University Press.

Gorz, A. (1965), 'Work and consumption', in P. Anderson and R. Blackburn (eds), *Towards Socialism*, London, Collins.

Gorz, A. (1982), *Farewell to the Working Class*, London, Pluto.

Gouldner, A.W. (1954), *Patterns of Industrial Bureaucracy*, New York, Free Press.

Grazia, R. De (1984), *Clandestine Employment: The Situation in the Industrialised Market Economy Countries*, Geneva, International Labour Office.

Gutmann, P.M. (1977), 'The subterranean economy', *Financial Analysts Journal*, November/December: 26–7 and 34.

Hakim, C. (1979), 'Occupational segregation', *Research Paper No. 9*, London, Department of Employment.

Hakim, C. (1980), 'Homeworking: some new evidence', *Employment Gazette*, vol. 88: 1105–10.

Hakim, C. (1984), 'Homework and outwork: national estimates from two surveys', *Employment Gazette*, vol. 92: 7–12.

Hakim, C. (1985), 'Employers' use of outwork. A study using the 1980 Workplace Industrial Relations Survey and the 1981 National Survey of Homeworking', *Research Paper No. 44*, London, Department of Employment.

Hakim, C. (1987), 'Home-based work in Britain', *Research Paper No. 60*, London, Department of Employment.

Hakim, C. and Dennis, R. (1982), 'Homeworking in wages councils industries', *Research Paper No. 37*, London, Department of Employment.

Handy, C. (1982), 'The informal economy: an essay on contemporary opportunities and challenges', *ARVAC Pamphlet No. 3*, ARVAC, Wivenhoe.

Handy, C. (1984), *The Future of Work: A Guide to a Changing Society*, Oxford, Basil Blackwell.

Harris, C.C. (1983), *The Family and Industrial Society*, London, George Allen and Unwin.

Harris, C.C., Lee, R.M. and Morris, L.D. (1985), 'Redundancy in steel:

labour market behaviour, local social networks and domestic organisation', in B. Roberts, R. Finnegan and D. Gallie (eds), *New Approaches to Economic Life: Economic Restructuring: Unemployment and the Social Division of Labour*, Manchester, Manchester University Press.

Harris, C.C. and the Redundancy and Unemployment Research Group (1987), *Redundancy and Recession in South Wales*, Oxford, Basil Blackwell.

Hart, K. (1973), 'Informal income opportunities and urban employment in Ghana', *Journal of Modern African Studies*, vol. 11: 61–89.

Hartley, J. (1987), 'Managerial unemployment: the wife's perspective and role', in S. Fineman, (ed.), *Unemployment, Personal and Social Consequences*, London, Tavistock.

Heertje, A., Allen, M. and Cohen, H. (1982), *The Black Economy: How it Works, Who it Works and What it Costs*, London, Pan Books.

Henderson, P. and Thomas, D.N. (eds) (1981), *Readings in Community Work*, London, George Allen and Unwin.

Henry, J. (1976), 'Calling in the big bills', *Washington Monthly*, May.

Henry, S. (1978), *The Hidden Economy: The Context and Control of Borderline Crime*, Oxford, Martin Robertson.

Henry, S. (ed) (1981), *Can I Have It In Cash? A Study of Informal Institutions and Unorthodox Ways of Doing Things*, London, Astragal Books.

Henry, S. (1982), 'The working unemployed: perspectives on the informal economy and unemployment', *Sociological Review*, vol. 30: 460–77.

Henry, S. and Mars, G. (1978), 'Crime at work: the social construction of amateur property theft', *Sociology*, vol. 12: 245–63.

Hess, H. (1973), *Mafia and Mafiosi: The Structure of Power*, London, Saxon House.

Hoggett, P. and Bishop, H. (1985), *Organising around Enthusiasms: Mutual Aid in Leisure*, London, Comedia.

Howe, L. (1984), 'The unemployed on supplementary benefit', *Scope*, no. 76: 12–14.

Howe, L. (1985a), 'The "deserving" and the "undeserving": practice in an urban, local Social Security Office', *Journal of Social Policy*, vol. 14: 49–72.

Howe, L. (1985b), 'Unemployment: historical aspects of data collection and the black economy in Belfast', presented to the annual conference of the Association of Social Anthropologists.

Howe, L. (1987), 'Doing the double: wages, jobs and benefits in Belfast', paper presented to conference on 'Economic and Social Research in Northern Ireland', Belfast.

Hoyman, M. (1987), 'Female participation in the informal economy: a neglected issue', *The Annals of the American Academy of Political and Social Science*, vol. 493: 64–82.

Humble, S. (1982), *Voluntary Action in the 1980s: Summary of the Findings of the National Survey*, Berkhamsted, The Volunteer Centre.

Hutson, S. and Jenkins, R. (1987), 'Coming of age in South Wales', in P. Brown and D.N. Ashton (eds), *Education, Unemployment and Labour Markets*, Brighton, Falmer.

Huws, V. (1984), 'The new home-workers: new technology and the changing location of white-collar work', *Pamphlet No. 28*, London, Low Pay Unit.

Ianni, F.A.J. and Reuss-Ianni, E. (1972), *A Family Business*, London, Routledge and Kegan Paul.

Ianni, F.A.J. and Reuss-Ianni, E. (eds) (1976), *The Crime Society: Organized Crime and Corruption in America*, New York, Meridian.

Jahoda, M. (1982), *Employment and Unemployment: A Social-Psychological Analysis*, Cambridge, Cambridge University Press.

Jenkins, R. (1978), 'Doing a double', *New Society*, no. 811: 121.

Jenkins, R. (1982), 'Work and unemployment in industrial society: an anthropological perspective', in J. Laite (ed.) *Bibliographies on Local Labour Markets and the Informal Economy*, London, SSRC.

Jenkins, R. (1983), *Lads, Citizens and Ordinary Kids: Working Class Youth Lifestyles in Belfast*, London, Routledge and Kegan Paul.

Jenkins, R. (1984a), 'Bringing it all back home: an anthropologist in Belfast', in C. Bell and H. Roberts (eds), *Social Researching*, London, Routledge and Kegan Paul.

Jenkins, R. (1984b), 'Ethnic minorities in business: a research agenda', in R. Ward and R. Jenkins (eds), *Ethnic Communities in Business: Strategies for Economic Survival*, Cambridge, Cambridge University Press.

Jenkins, R. (1986), *Racism and Recruitment: Managers, Organisations and Equal Opportunity in the Labour Market*, Cambridge, Cambridge University Press.

Joshi, H. (1984), 'Women's participation in paid work', *Research Paper No. 45*, London, Department of Employment.

Katsenelinboigen, A. (1977), 'Coloured markets in the Soviet Union', *Soviet Studies*, vol. 29: 62–85.

Kerr, C., Dunlop, J.T., Harbison, F. and Myers, C.A. (1973), *Industrialism and Industrial Man*, second edition, Harmondsworth, Pelican.

Kilpatrick, R. and Trew, K. (1985), 'Life-styles and psychological well-being among unemployed men in Northern Ireland', *Journal of Occupational Psychology*, vol. 58: 207–16.

Klockars, C.B. (1974), *The Professional Fence*, London, Tavistock.

Kumar, K. (1978), *Prophecy and Progress: The Sociology of Industrial and Post-Industrial Society*, London, Allen Lane.

Land, H. (1981), *Parity Begins at Home: Women's and Men's Work in the Home and its Effect on their Paid Employment*, Manchester/London, EOC/SSRC.

Lee, R.M. (1985), 'Dejeopardizing techniques for asking sensitive questions on survey: applications from the study of the black economy', unpublished paper, Department of Sociology and Anthropology, University College, Swansea.

Leighton, P. (1983), 'Contractual arrangements in selected industries: a study of employment relationships in industries with outwork', *Research Paper No. 39*, London, Department of Employment.

Lemert, E.M. (1972), *Human Deviance, Social Problems and Social Control*, Englewood Cliffs, NJ, Prentice-Hall.

Leonard, D. (1980), *Sex and Generation: A Study of Courtship and Weddings*, London, Tavistock.

Liebow, E. (1967), *Tally's Corner*, Boston, Little, Brown.

Lipsig-Mumme, C. (1973), 'The renaissance of home-working in developed economies', *Industrial Relations Quarterly Review*, vol. 38: 545–67.

Long, N. (ed) (1984), *Family and Work in Rural Societies: Perspectives on Non-Wage Labour*, London, Tavistock.

Macafee, K. (1980), 'A glimpse of the hidden economy in the national accounts', *Economic Trends*, February: 81–7.

Mackie, L. and Pattullo, P. (1977), *Women and Work*, London, Tavistock.

Marcuse, H. (1968), *One Dimensional Man*, London, Sphere.

Mars, G. (1973), 'Hotel pilferage: a case study in occupational theft', in M. Warner (ed.), *The Sociology of the Work Place*, London, Allen and Unwin.

Mars, G. (1974), 'Dock pilferage', in P. Rock and M. McIntosh (eds), *Deviance and Control*, London, Tavistock.

Mars, G. (1979), 'The stigma cycle: values and politics in a dockland union', in S. Wallman (ed.), *Social Anthropology of Work*, London, Academic Press.

Mars, G. (1982), *Cheats at Work: An Anthropology of Workplace Crime*, London, Allen and Unwin.

Mars, G. and Nicod, M. (1984), *The World of Waiters*, London, Allen and Unwin.

Martin, J. and Roberts C. (1984), *Women and Employment: A Lifetime Perspective*, London, HMSO.

Martin, R. and Wallace, J. (1984), *Working Women in Recession: Employment, Redundancy and Unemployment*, Oxford, Oxford University Press.

Mattera, P. (1985), *Off the Books: The Rise of the Underground Economy*, London, Pluto Press.

Matthews, K. (1983), 'National income and the black economy', *Economic Affairs*, July: 261–7.

Matthews, K. and Rastogi, A. (1985), 'Little Mo and the moonlighter: another look at the black economy', Liverpool Research Group on Macroeconomics, *Quarterly Economic Bulletin*, vol. 6, no. 2.

McIntosh, M. (1975), *The Organisation of Crime*, London, Macmillan.

McKee, L. and Bell, C. (1985), 'Marital and family relationships in times of male unemployment', in B. Roberts, R. Finnegan and D. Gallie (eds), *New Approaches in Economic Life: Economic Restructuring: Unemployment and the Social Division of Labour*, Manchester, Manchester University Press.

Merton, R.K. (1957), *Social Theory and Social Structure*, revised edition, New York, Free Press.

Miller, R. (1979) 'Evidence of attitudes to evasion from a sample survey', in A. Seldon (ed.), *Tax Avoision*, London, Institute of Economic Affairs.

Miller, W.B. (1958), 'Lower-class culture as a generating milieu of gang delinquency', *Journal of Social Issues*, vol. 14: 5–19.

Mingione, E. (1985), 'Social reproduction of the surplus labour force: the case of Southern Italy', in N. Redclift and E. Mingione (eds), *Beyond Employment: Household, Gender and Subsistence*, Oxford, Basil Blackwell.

Molyneux, M. (1979), 'Beyond the domestic labour debate', *New Left*

Review, no. 116: 3–27.

Morris, L.D. (1983), 'Local social networks and post-redundancy labour-market experience', working paper, University College, Swansea.

Morris, L.D. (1984), 'Patterns of social activity and post-redundancy labour-market experience', *Sociology*, vol. 18: 339–52.

Morris, L.D. (1985), 'Renegotiation of the domestic division of labour in the context of male redundancy', in B. Roberts, R. Finnegan and D. Gallie (eds), *New Approaches to Economic Life: Economic Restructuring: Unemployment and the Social Division of Labour*, Manchester, Manchester University Press.

Morris, L.D. (1987), 'Local social polarization: a case study of Hartlepool', *International Journal of Urban and Regional Research*, vol. 11: 331–50.

Morris, T.P. (1957), *The Criminal Area: A Study in Social Ecology*, London, Routledge and Kegan Paul.

Morrissey, M., O'Connor, T.P. and Tipping, B. (1984), 'Doing the double in Northern Ireland', *Social Studies*, vol. 8, nos 1/2: 41–54.

Myrdal, A. and Klein, V. (1968), *Women's Two Roles: Home and Work*, second edition, London, Routledge and Kegan Paul.

Nelli, H.S. (1976), *The Business of Crime: Italians and Syndicate Crime in the United States*, New York, Oxford University Press.

Newby, H., Bell, C., Rose, D. and Saunders, P. (1978), *Property, Paternalism and Power: Class and Control in Rural England*, London, Hutchinson.

Oakley, A. (1974a), *Housewife*, London, Allen Lane.

Oakley, A. (1974b), *The Sociology of Housework*, Oxford, Martin Robertson.

O'Higgins, M. (1980), *Measuring the Hidden Economy: A Review of Evidence and Methodologies*, London, Outer Circle Policy Unit.

Ong, W.J. (1982) *Orality and Literacy: The Technologizing of the Word*, London, Methuen.

Outer Circle Policy Unit, (n.d.), *Policing the Hidden Economy*, London, Outer Circle Policy Unit.

Pahl, R.E. (1980), 'Employment, work and the domestic division of labour', *International Journal of Urban and Regional Research*, vol. 4: 1–20.

Pahl, R.E. (1984), *Divisions of Labour*, Oxford, Basil Blackwell.

Pahl, R.E. (1986), Review of P. Hoggett and J. Bishop, *Organizing around Enthusiasms*, *New Society*, no. 1221: 30–1.

Pahl, R.E. (1987), 'Does jobless mean workless? Unemployment and informal work', *The Annals of the American Academy of Political and Social Science*, vol. 493: 36–46.

Pahl, R.E. (1988), 'Some remarks on informal work, social polarization and the social structure', *International Journal of Urban and Regional Research*, vol. 12: 247–67.

Pahl, R.E. and Wallace, C. (1985), 'Household work strategies in economic recession', in N. Redclift and E. Mingione (eds), *Beyond Employment: Household, Gender and Subsistence*, Oxford, Basil Blackwell.

Pantaleone, M. (1966), *The Mafia and Politics*, London, Chatto and Windus.

Parker, H. (1974), *View from the Boys*, Newton Abbot, David and Charles.

Parker, S. (1983), *Leisure and Work*, London, George Allen and Unwin.

Pinnaro, G. and Pugliese, E. (1985), 'Informalization and social resistance: the case of Naples', in N. Redclift and E. Mingione (eds),

Beyond Employment: Household, Gender and Subsistence, Oxford, Basil Blackwell.

Pollert, A. (1981), *Girls, Wives, Factory Lives*, London, Macmillan.

Polsky, N. (1967), *Hustlers, Beats and Others*, Harmondsworth, Penguin.

Popay, J. (1985), 'Women, the family and unemployment', in P. Close and R. Collins (eds), *Family and Economy in Modern Society*, London, Macmillan.

Portes, A. and Sassen-Koob, S. (1987), 'Making it underground: comparative material on the informal sector in western market economies', *American Journal of Sociology*, vol. 93: 30–61.

President's Commission on Law Enforcement and Administration of Justice (1967), *Task Force Report: Crime and its Impact – An Assessment*, Washington, D.C., Government Printing Office.

Pryce, K. (1979), *Endless Pressure: A Study of West Indian Life-styles in Britain*, Harmondsworth, Penguin.

Punch, M. (1979), *Policing the Inner City: A Study of Amsterdam's Warmoestraat*, London, Macmillan.

Redclift, N. and Mingione, E. (eds) (1985), *Beyond Employment: Household, Gender and Subsistence*, Oxford, Basil Blackwell.

Rees, A.D. (1951), *Life in a Welsh Countryside*, Cardiff, University of Wales Press.

Reynolds, F. (1986), *The Problem Housing Estate*, Aldershot, Gower.

Reynolds, F., Duffy, F. and Harding, P. (1983), *All Mod Cons: A Study of a 'Problem' Housing Estate*, unpublished report to the Joseph Rowntree Memorial Trust.

Richmond, A.H. (1988), *Immigration and Ethnic Conflict*, London, Macmillan.

Rojek, C. (1985), *Capitalism and Leisure Theory*, London, Tavistock.

Roldan, M. (1985), 'Industrial outworking, struggle for reproduction of working class families and gender subordination', in N. Redclift and E. Mingione (eds), *Beyond Employment: Household, Gender and Subsistence*, Oxford, Basil Blackwell.

Rose, M. (1975), *Industrial Behaviour: Theoretical Developments since Taylor*, London, Allen Lane.

Rose, R. (1985), 'Getting by in three economies: the resources of the official, unofficial and domestic economies', in J. Lane (ed.), *State and Market: The Politics of the Public and the Private*, London, Sage.

Rosser, C. and Harris, C.C. (1965), *The Family and Social Change: A Study of Family and Kinship in a South Wales Town*, London, Routledge and Kegan Paul.

Rubery, J. and Wilkinson, F. (1981), 'Outwork and segmented labour markets', in F. Wilkinson (ed.), *The Dynamics of Labour Market Segmentation*, London, Academic Press.

Rushton, P. (1979), 'Marxism, domestic labour and capitalist economy', in C.C. Harris (ed.), 'The sociology of the family: new directions for Britain', *Sociological Review Monograph no. 28*, Keele, Sociological Review.

Sahlins, M. (1974), *Stone Age Economics*, London, Tavistock.

Salaman, G. (1979), *Work Organisations: Resistance and Control*, London, Longman.

Scase, R. and Goffee, R. (1980), *The Real World of the Small Business Owner*, London, Croom Helm.

Schur, E.M. (1971), *Labeling Deviant Behaviour: Its Sociological Implications*, Englewood Cliffs, NJ, Prentice-Hall.

Shaw, C. and McKay, H. (1969), *Juvenile Delinquency in Urban Areas*, 2nd edition, Chicago, Chicago University Press.

Silverman, D. and Jones, J. (1976), *Organizational Work*, London, Collier-Macmillan.

Simon, H.A. (1957), *Administrative Behaviour: A Study of Decision-Making Processes in Administration Organisation*, second edition, New York, Free Press.

Sirken, M.G., Indefurth, G.T., Burnham, C.E. and Danchik, K.M. (1975), 'Household sample surveys of diabetes: design effect and counting rules', *Proceedings of the American Statistical Society: Social Statistics Section*, pp. 659–63.

Smith, J.D. (1987), 'Measuring the informal economy', *The Annals of the American Academy of Political and Social Science*, vol. 493: 83–99.

Smith, S. (1986), *Britain's Shadow Economy*, Oxford, Clarendon Press.

Smith, S. and Wied-Nebbeling, S. (1986), *The Shadow Economy in Britain and Germany*, London, Anglo-German Foundation.

Smithies, E. (1984), *The Black Economy in England since 1914*, Dublin, Gill and Macmillan.

South, N. and Scratton, P. (1981), 'Capitalist discipline, private justice and the hidden economy', *Occasional Paper no. 2*, Centre for Occupational and Community Research, Middlesex Polytechnic, Enfield.

Stack, C.B. (1974), *All Our Kin: Strategies for Survival in a Black Community*, New York, Harper and Row.

Stedman Jones, G. (1984), *Outcast London*, revised edition, Harmondsworth, Peregrine.

Street, B.V. (1984), *Literacy in Theory and Practice*, Cambridge, Cambridge University Press.

Sutherland, E.H. (1949), *White Collar Crime*, New York, Dryden.

Suttles, G.D. (1968), *The Social Order of the Slum*, Chicago, University of Chicago Press.

Tambs-Lyche, H. (1980), *London Patidars: A Case in Urban Ethnicity*, London, Routledge and Kegan Paul.

Tanzi, V. (1980), 'Underground economy and tax evasion in the United States', *Banca Nazionale del Lavoro Quarterly Review*, December.

Tanzi, V. (1982), 'A second (more sceptical) look at the underground economy in the United States', in V. Tanzi (ed.), *The Underground Economy in the United States and Abroad*, Lexington, Mass, Lexington Books.

The Times (1983), 'Fighting the counterfeiters', 27 October.

Thomas, J.J. (1988), 'The politics of the black economy', *Work, Employment and Society*, vol. 2: 169–90.

Thomas, M. (1969), *The Fire Service and its Personnel*, London, HMSO.

Tipping, B. (1982), 'Scrounging in Northern Ireland: the beginnings of an investigation', *Economic and Social Review*, vol. 13: 217–32.

Titmuss, R.M. (1970), *The Gift Relationship: From Human Blood to Social Policy*, London, George Allen and Unwin.

Touraine, A. (1974), *The Post-Industrial Society*, London, Wildwood House.

Trew. K. and Kilpatrick, R. (1984), *The Daily Life of the Unemployed: Social and Psychological Dimensions*, Department of Psychology, Queen's University of Belfast, Belfast.

Turner, B.A. (1971), *Exploring the Industrial Subculture*, London, Macmillan.

Turner, R., Bostyn, A. and Wight, D. (1985), 'The work ethic in a Scottish town with declining employment', in B. Roberts, R. Finnegan and D. Gallie (eds), *New Approaches to Economic Life: Economic Restructuring: Unemployment and the Social Division of Labour*, Manchester, Manchester University Press.

Twelvetrees, A. (1982), *Community Work*, London, Macmillan.

Urry, J. (1981), *The Anatomy of Capitalist Societies: The Economy, Civil Society and the State*, London, Macmillan.

US Congress, Joint Economic Committee (1983), *Growth of the Underground Economy 1950–81*, Washington, DC, Government Printing Office.

US Congress, Senate Committee on Governmental Affairs, Permanent Sub-committee on Investigations (1980), *Illegal Narcotics Profits*, Hearings held 7, 11, 12, 13 and 14 December 1979, Washington, DC, Government Printing Office.

US Congress, Senate Committee on Governmental Affairs, Permanent Sub-committee on Investigations (1983), *Crime and Secrecy: The Use of Offshore Banks and Companies*, Washington, DC, Government Printing Office.

US Internal Revenue Service (1979), *Estimates of Income Unreported on Individual Income Tax Returns*, Washington, DC, Government Printing Office.

US Internal Revenue Service (1983), *Income Tax Compliance Research: Estimates for 1973–1981*, Washington, DC, Government Printing Office.

Vickerman, R.W. (1980), 'The new leisure society – an economic analysis', *Futures*, vol. 12: 191–200.

Wadel, C. (1973), *Now, Whose Fault is That?*, Institute of Social and Economic Research, Memorial University of Newfoundland, St John's.

Wadel, C. (1979), 'The hidden work of everyday life', in S. Wallman (ed.), *Social Anthropology of Work*, London, Academic Press.

Wall Street Journal (1976), 'Organized bootlegging by northern states hurt by tax-revenue loss', 15 September.

Wallace, C. (1986), 'From girls and boys to women and men', in S. Walker and L. Barton (eds), *Youth, Unemployment and Schooling*, Milton Keynes, Open University Press.

Walsh, S. (1981), 'The manufacture of excitement in police–juvenile encounters', *British Journal of Criminology*, vol. 21: 257–67.

Walton, R.G. (ed.) (1986), 'Integrating formal and informal care – the utilization of social support networks', *British Journal of Social Work*, vol. 16, supplement.

Ward, R. and Jenkins, R. (eds), (1984), *Ethnic Communities in Business:*

Strategies for Economic Survival, Cambridge, Cambridge University Press.

Weber, M. (1978), *Economy and Society*, eds G. Roth and C. Wittig, Berkeley, University of California Press.

Weiss, L. (1987), 'Explaining the underground economy: state and social structure', *British Journal of Sociology*, vol. xxxviii: 216–34.

Whyte, W.F. (1955), *Street Corner Society*, second edition, Chicago, University of Chicago Press.

Williams, W.M. (1956), *The Sociology of an English Village: Gosforth*, London, Routledge and Kegan Paul.

Willmott, P. (1986), *Social Networks, Informal Care and Public Policy*, London, Policy Studies Institute.

Willmott, P. (1987), *Friendship Networks and Social Support*, London, Policy Studies Institute.

Yeager, M.G. (1976), 'The gangster as white collar criminal', in F.A.J. Ianni and E. Reuss-Ianni (eds), *The Crime Society*, New York, Meridian Books.

Yeandle, S. (1984), *Women's Working Lives*, London, Tavistock.

Young, M. and Willmott, P. (1957), *Family and Kinship in East London*, London, Routledge and Kegan Paul.

Author Index

SUBJECT INDEX

Note: There are a number of topics or subjects which, because they occur throughout the book, have not been separately indexed. Examples are 'informal economic activity' and 'United Kingdom'. Nor have we attempted to index the plethora of nomenclature and colour-coding which characterizes the confusion of the *ad hoc* model-building of the 'separate economies' debate.